T0209917

NOTES FROM A BOTTLE FOUND ON THE BEACH AT CARMEL

notes from a bottle found on the beach at carmel

EVAN S. CONNELL

COUNTERPOINT

BERKELEY

Library of Congress Cataloging-in-Publication is available.
ISBN 978-1-61902-052-8

Cover design by Ann Weinstock
Interior design by Domini Dragoone

COUNTERPOINT
2560 Ninth Street, Suite 318
Berkeley, CA 94710
www.counterpointpress.com

Printed in the United States of America

10 9 8 7 6 5 4 3 2

TO MAX STEELE

There be many shapes of mystery,
And many things God makes to be,
Past hope or fear.
And the end men looked for
Cometh not,
And a path is there where no man sought.
So hath it fallen here.
Euripides

Pater noster, qui es in cœlis: sanctificetur nomen tuum.
Adveniat regnum tuum. Fiat voluntas tua, sicut in cœlo,
et in terra.

There was a platform in the center of the court
and on this lay Damiens, his body bound
with iron hoops. First, his right hand was thrust
into a sulphurous fire;
he uttered a frightful shriek. Next
they attacked him with glowing tongs
and tore away strips of bleeding flesh.
Molten lead, wax, pitch, and burning oil
were poured into the wounds,
and a team of horses was summoned to dismember him.
But although the animals were whipped and spurred
they were not strong enough.
Two more horses were affixed to the chains
so that finally the left leg of Damiens was sucked
out of its socket and wrenched loose from his body
while the people cheered. The next limb to be torn . . .

Mon frère, a-t-il tout ce qu'il veut?
Has my brother everything he needs?

To what prayer will you listen, if not to this?

One heart, one way.

There is a day of the year
when eels go down to the Sargasso Sea. And I
must go with them. Come with me,
or stay.

11

I am full of dreams and charged with a strange excitement!
Although I am not at ease in this world, there is no one
who can stop me!

I met a man who said that he was on the road to Córdoba.
But he said to me that he never would reach Córdoba.
I asked him why
and he explained that Death was watching him.
Death was gazing down on him from the towers of Córdoba.

Whenever the barrel is turned, the crystals tumble.

The first Ch'in Divine August One
learned, to his satisfaction and to his dismay,
that he had conquered every civilized land;
for he believed that beyond the borders of his empire
nothing existed but howling winds and barren waste.
At this same time Alexander
had overrun the Western World. So it was
that two men not knowing of the existence of each other
shared a common delusion.

Someone just now has touched me! A human hand
has touched me! — I am ill and I need to lie down.

In the land of the Tepehuane on the floor of a canyon
somewhere in the Sierra Madre are three things:
a silver mine, the white ruins of a hacienda,
and a grove of orange trees. The mine is called
El Naranjal, after the orange grove, and whoever
can find it will be rich for the rest of his life;
his children after him, and theirs after them.
Every so often, down a certain river whose origins
are lost among the peaks of the Sierra Madre,
an orange comes floating. Then it is that

men look to the mountains and begin to dream,
for they know this orange has come from the grove
where the great mine is; and all night long
they lie awake beside their drowsy wives,
thinking of the bright morning when they shall
enter into distant mountains to discover El Naranjal.

Direct us, O God! We must find the way, or we are lost.

Nunc lento sonitu dicunt, morieris.
Now this bell, tolling softly for another,
says to us that we must die.

We are 8 Goths and 22 Norwegians
on a journey of exploration
from Vinland around the west.
By a lake with 2 skerries
one day's travel north from
this stone we made camp. One day
we fished. We came home and
there were 10 of our men red
with blood and dead. Ave Virgo
Maria. Save us from evil. We have
10 men by the sea to protect our
ships 14 days' travel from this
island in the year of Our Saviour
1362.

Things that remain and are not diminished by time
are whichever live in men's hearts, or have fallen
or have been thrown into the sea.

It is well known that in Mare Tenebrosum
sea creatures with fins heavier than bronze
disport themselves, while the waters of the equator

spout upwards in hideous black jets. There
no caravel is safe. *Pater noster, qui es . . .*

In the sky over Brittany a blazing thing
like a globe has been seen.
On its beams a wreath of fire hangs
like the breath of a dragon, out of which proceed
two astral rays. And of these,
one is manifest in France
while the other stretches to Ireland!

We know that only through observation or by
the sense of touch are we able to recognize and identify
the handiwork of our brothers, in this way
distinguishing it from prodigies of natural force.

Dark diamonds of Hindustan, figured silks
from Lahore,
flame of Fusi-yama. Someone has touched me!

It is as though I am in a palatial home
not far from the sea, although I do not know
which sea. Or is it a river? My companions
are at the table and I will soon join them;
but at this instant I am holding in my left hand
a photograph of my father, who has been dead for
many years. I was not even aware that I owned
this picture. When the photograph was taken
he was the age I am while I compose these apothegms.
Like me, he wears a luxuriant mustache
curled up at the ends. Indeed, we resemble
twin brothers who comb their hair differently
in order to be distinguished. Yet he smiles,
he is more amenable; we are not the same.
I shall place his picture in my valise

and go and make conversation with my friends,
 but I will not mention this moment.
To think deeply right now would terrify me.

Murder is born of fright and hatred,
anxiety, desperation, jealousy and greed,
spite, humiliation and resentment. Of these
and more, which all are within the compass of Mankind,
has not love been found?

Through the lemon trees a light rain is falling and
early snow delicately sifts on the mountain.

Another flake has fallen through the years.

She is dead, the flower of April.
She is dead, the flower of May.
She is gone, she is dead,
she who reigned in the royal palace of Madrid.
Donde vas, Rey Alfonsito? Where goest thou
thus sadly?

They built a long bronze dais
on which they laid out an embossed map of the empire
showing each palace, ministry, village, and hamlet,
all in miniature. Each river
and tributary was of mercury,
and the sea also;
and the tributaries flowed into the rivers
and the rivers flowed into the sea.
The vault was painted to represent the firmament,
and they lighted the tomb with fish oil in golden tanks
and laid him in his sarcophagus,
he who was master of the world.
But soon a thief had found the entrance,

pried open the lid of the sarcophagus
and tore away the wrappings, drew the rings
from his fingers, and stole the emeralds
which were his eyes.

Whatever remains undiminished
by time must live in men's hearts,
be thrown, or have fallen
into the sea.

Saint Nicholas of Tolentino restored to life
the doves that were brought to him as delicacies.

Riddle, fable, enigma, allegory, and acrostic we employ
in order to confound the obtuse, the profane and clumsy,
for whom all wisdom is no more than means to their end.
*M. the azothi acefth epuhiloqosophersa lisati ptheiruri
imeracurerty.* The azoth is the beginning; the rest
shall be left in mystery. Do not assume your light is
inviolable. *Visita Interiora Terræ Rectificando
Invenies Occultum Lapidem*—thus may vitriol be written.

The conviction that it is possible to transmute
one substance into another is derived from
the hypothesis of the unicity of matter.
In the same way, we believe the delinquency of Man
 may be subject to transmutation. If this is so,
no pilgrimage should be considered vain.

I shall make the most of winter;
who can announce the date of spring?

Paradise is toward the East
and in Paradise is a tree
called the Mandragora,

which springs from human sperm
that is spilt on the ground.

I know Paradise is real which we have lost
but find again through the gates of memory.

Thoughts of love
visit me rarely.

Do you know me? Do you know my heart? I have offered
my green porcelain bowl
to buy flowers for a strange woman.

On a Sumerian cylinder I have read an inscription
which tells of a woman
fashioned out of a rib; and of Enki and Ninhursag,
who lived in earthly bliss
surrounded by forbidden fruits,
who fell from grace
not by the low cunning of a serpent
but through the wiles of a fox.

Eden is derived from the Babylonian word, *edinu.*

Now it is afternoon; the water has become
the color of Persian ceramic—that utter blue we find
within the tiles of the Grand Mosque of Achmet.

There was a moment when clouds lifted above Pomègue
whose name, she whispered, was taken from Phœnicia.
Its waters were clear and shallow and I
beheld a sandy bed, strewn with statuary and amphoræ;
and I was gazing down when she murmured that her husband
waited on the quai, but we might have a moment together
if I wished.

Days cannot occur together, nor times exist at once.

She seemed to believe love always existed;
subjugation, indolence, assurance—leisurely gestures
seldom explained. I could not begin to guess
how old she was. What did it matter?
I thought of Domitian and Retiarius, of Secutor
and young men calculating how soon, how intimately
they should fondle her.

Two in the morning.
The moon pours across the tropic sea
its useless beauty.
Should I have followed her,
or not ? And are we figures from the Red King's dream,
dissolving as He wakes?

Tatuantinsuyu!
Abide in me
four quarters of the earth.

Each life is a myth, a song given out
of darkness, a tale for children, the legend we create.
Are we not heroes, each of us
in one fashion or another,
wandering through mysterious labyrinths?

I have dreamt of Tamurlane and Kubilai Khan!

Ecce signum; behold
this proof.

The Tartars do not care what god is worshiped;
each man is free to do as he wills about his soul,
only so long as j ustice is observed. They hold

that while Jesus Christ may be a great lord,
he is a proud lord who will not keep company
with others, but needs to rule the earth.
For this reason they do not highly honor him.

It is said the people of the mountains above Ferlac
worship many things. But whatever they first behold
in the morning light—that is what they worship.

I must establish beyond doubt
the inconceivable purity of my intent.

Some say the tuna swims around the world
searching for a better life because he is not at home
in the sea. It may be we have met, this obsessed fish
and I, somewhere beyond the Pillars of Hercules.

Each journey is the consequence of unbearable longing.

I am looking for my brother.
Have you seen him?
Has he come this way?

Bohemund, a Christian, sent to the Greek emperor
a cargo of thumbs and noses. Pagans captured at Edessa
were crucified. I will speak of this again.
We are endowed with the capacity for unimaginable
suffering.

I have laid plans to reassert the sovereign individual
beyond the grasp and authority of his nation.
Nothing shall dissuade me from my purpose, nothing
save Death, but that would be enough.

Noon is the hour of greatest danger;

it is then one's shadow is least.
It is at noon that Pan appears.

Who can hear me?
Where should I turn?

My hatred of government exceeds the furthest imaginable
limit of human calculation. I am void of faith.
It is rumored—although no statement yet has been issued
from our capital—that an area equivalent to Switzerland
may be laid in ashes!

I despise the motility of crowds.

Pater de cœlis Deus, miserere Ludovici!
Fili redemptor . . .

We have entered the seventh millenary,
which is the conclusion, and brings us
near to the firmament of the eighth sphere,
which is the place where God shall make an end,
celestial bodies resume their motions.

Nothing existed before me; nothing will exist after me.

Because it is possible to have intuitive knowledge
of things which do not exist
our vision is absolute, distant in place and subject
from our object; and therefore visions remain,
as we witness a multitude of stars that have gone.

Thuban, which is also known as Alpha Draconis,
is located between Mizar, the horse,
and the ultimate stars of Ursa Minor. Now
when the Great Pyramid of Gizeh was built

this star, owing to the precession of the earth,
stood above the North Pole and was called Polaris.
But it is no longer so. Similarly
our pole star shall be ousted, while the moon
and planets, because they shine to our eyes by reason
of the brilliance of the sun, shall seem extinguished.
And on that day no clouds will form,
nor any snow fall. The atmosphere will liquefy
and freeze against the globe.
The absolute calm of eternity shall reign.

Without desire I call to mind each past desire;
all I have feared I now review, and find myself.

We are told by Aquinas in his *Summa Theologica*
that things which lack intelligence act toward an end;
which is evident from their always acting, or nearly so,
in a manner identical to obtain a desired result;
hence it becomes plain that not fortuitously,
but through design, do they achieve this end. Now
whatever lacks intelligence cannot move toward an end
unless it is directed there by some being endowed
with knowledge and intellect, as is the case
when an arrow is shot to its mark by the archer.

I have followed the cognate sciences,
I have followed mathematics with assiduity;
thus I have laid down the bounds and rules
according to which I enable myself
to develop everything that follows.

Between the dream and the act
I poise.

L'anima mi s'aggrandisce!

They told me I struggled with macabre ferocity
to preserve myself; and all who watched me
became subdued and apprehensive. They have said
I bit at the blankets in which a physician
had wrapped me, and there seemed another presence
in the room, for my eyes continually followed something
no one else could see. I spoke aloud—but in
an unknown tongue, and growled like a dog
which snaps at nothing. Then the air grew clearer,
as though some noxious vapor had been withdrawn,
and I shuddered and began to weep, and slept
six days without waking. Of all this, I remember naught.
Can there be another God, nearer to the heart?

Erasmus was ill, or thought he was, and so he sent for
Paracelsus, who wrote out for him an orthodox consilium.
To this Erasmus replied with much ceremony,
complimenting the alchemist on the diagnosis,
but seeing fit to add: *At present I have no time
for a cure, indeed I have not the time either to be sick
or to die, because I am engaged in exacting studies.*

Now, Paracelsus was a curious man. And he
bore a most curious name: Phillipus Theophrastus
Aureolus Bombastus ab Hohenheim, Eremita. There have
been better men, there have been worse. Some claim
he was Faustus. Whether this is true, no one knows.
But Isaac Newton believed that in those days in Bohemia
it was possible to transmute iron into copper.
At any rate, when Theophrastus had finished working
in the Venetian mercury mines of Dalmatia
he returned to his father's house, bringing with him
the drug laudanum, and an enormous sword.
From this sword he was not ever parted for the rest of
his life, not even in sleep. Now, the black hellebore

blossoms in winter, and it was Paracelsus
who introduced this plant into pharmacy,
recommending it to persons fifty years of age and over;
and, as it turned out, the dosage he prescribed
is the correct amount to alleviate the symptoms of
arteriosclerosis. Paracelsus, however,
cautioned that hellebore should be gathered only
beneath a full moon. His familiar heard him mutter
as he lay dying: *I have traveled through this land*
and was a pilgrim all my life, alone, and a stranger
feeling alien. Then Thou hast made grow in me Thine art
under the breath of the terrible storm in me.
This is why the name of Theophrastus of Hohenheim
comes down to Mankind through the course of centuries.

According to Boethius, we are attracted by likeness
but repelled by diversity; therefore it follows
that whatever seeks a thing outside itself must be
of that same nature which it seeks.

The Mandragora shrieks when uprooted from the earth;
every mortal man who hears this sound goes mad.

Visions are not without their usage, however fanciful,
if only to purge us of dark and sickening forms.

Dead is the dead Albigensian,
Vaudois,
Moor,
Jew,
and Indian.
Let this be recorded!

The victim is escorted to the marketplace.
He is rigidly bound.

A surgeon slits the palm of each hand in four places,
the slits are packed with salt
and each hand is pressed shut
with the fingertips forced into the slits,
the hands being maintained in this position
by the use of gloves cut from wet oxhide
which shrinks as it dries.
The victim next is carried to his cell
where he is fed and attended with solicitude
closely guarded to prevent his suicide,
so that he may live to experience his agony
and thus repent. Whatever follows
may be considered appropriate to our time.

It seemed to us he made frantic efforts
to leap up—to escape our fabulous chair.
The leather creaked and groaned
and appeared to yield, but held him securely.
He slavered and snapped, writhing ferociously. Amazed
were we who stared at his hands contorted into fists;
we looked also at the top of his forehead
above the painted mask. It was red as a spring rose.
Around the bright edge of his metal cap the hair
stood straight out, as stiff as quills.
We heard a buzzing noise and thought
a swarm of wasps had flown into the chamber
while threads of smoke curled above him.

Commiseration was,
and is,
unwise; whoever is shown
to sympathize
must of himself
be guilty.
I am Magus.

Trust in me.

Seven thousand at Trèves. Brighter
than the midday sun at Hiroshima.

I am searching for my brother. Have you seen him?

The character of an organization,
like that of an individual,
shall be tested when some man or
principle is found which stands
irrevocably in opposition.
Hier stehe ich, ich kann nicht anders.

Just now the wireless brings news of a world
we have nearly forgotten:
in the jungle the wreckage of an aircraft has been found.
Blue stars and moons are painted on its wings, and
clothed in the tatters of a uniform
a skeleton sits at the controls, the skull resting
on the collarbone, as though lost in meditation.

I foresee
such a struggle between them
because they are grown
so equal in savagery
they will be separated
by nothing
less than Death.

Possessed by the sequence of my thought,
I am aware that to contemplate its possibilities
would prove fatal.

Signa autem obsidentis dæmonis sunt:

ignota lingua loqui pluribus verbis, vel
loquentem intelligere; distantia et
occulta patefacere; vires supra ætatis
seu conditionis naturam ostendere.
The specific signs of Possession are
these: use or understanding of an
unknown tongue; knowledge of distant
or hidden facts . . .

Twilight in Alicante. I take the flight
of a bat for the passage of the Evil One.

I discard the learning of my age
to achieve a higher knowledge. I would
wait for you, but there is so little time.
Adjutorium nostrum in nomine Domini . . .

Cologne, famed queen of darkness! Albertus Magnus declares
sage placed in a fountain brings thunder and lightning.

Three women of Strassburg who, at the same instant,
felt themselves kicked, although no one else was near,
accused a certain man, weeping and declaring he
had cast a spell on them; whereupon he was bound over
to torture, but saved himself by means of a lie,
saying indeed he had kicked out—though not at
three Christian women, but at three cats which savagely
attacked him. This is the reason he was freed
but the women burnt. Here is a parable of our time.

Ahasuerus, with the gift of prevision, is
obligated to suffer his agony thrice—
in anticipation, actuality, and recollection.

How many churches count among their priceless relics

the prepuce of Jesus Christ? The answer is twelve.

It is said the cuttlefish avoids pursuit by troubling
the water, making his neighborhood as black as ink;
the same is true of Man. Thus, the act of copulation
is held to be illegal on Sunday, Wednesday, and
Friday. It is illegal for a period of forty days
prior to Easter and to Christmas, and for three days
prior to Communion. It is forbidden from the time of
conception till forty days after parturition.
According to some, the consequence of these restrictions
is phantasmagoria, looming, flagellation, and slavering,
while others assert these constitute satanic seizures.

Ogni vero non è buono a dire.
By virtue of suppression do we lie.

The physician of imperial Rome was Galen,
known to many as Paradoxopœus.
It was he who concocted theriac,
 which is the antidote to every poison,
except the poison of the mind.

The moon climbs and follows its ordained path
with the fathoming probity of mathematics.

Quem colorem
habet sapientia?
What color
hath wisdom? Tell me,
if you know.

I have found a notebook filled with incomprehensible
and mysterious symbols—notes that pertain
to fearful discoveries.

I observe my shadow cast forward;
someone comes hurrying after me!
I listen, and hear my name
called down the years.
The corridor is alive with echoes.
To what use did Judas put his silver?

Last night I think I fainted in my sleep. There was blood
on my tongue this morning.

I remember an inn where I stayed overnight
and a door with a bronze lion's head,
with a ring in the mouth of the lion.
I was told I needed only to pull on this ring
to open the door. Eleven years have passed
and yet I cannot keep myself from wondering
what was there. A woman? A document? Or
a passage that led to another door?

Salvian complains that the causes of corruption
are not enticement, but exist within our hearts;
as also wickedness dwells not without, but in us.

Sodom and *Gomora* have been found
inscribed on the walls of a house
in Pompeii.

Now, I do not know if the man I met
is still on the road to Córdoba,
or if he has reached there.
Nor do I care. He has his life. I have mine.

I am not able to distinguish certain sounds—
those in which the letter M occurs—standing for
Millennium and the attendant revelations.

Particular odors and colors are lost to me, that earlier
I thought were valuable. Darkness settles toward us.
Like the embryo that recapitulates the race,
I live again the conflicts of my inheritance.

I have seen the last queen of the Gauls
dancing alone in a dark forest.
She wore a jeweled belt—emeralds
and sapphires encircled her waist,
and a dagger set with rubies
swung from a silver chain.
Her hair was long, it was as black
as Indian silk. Her necklace
was made of candle wax. Pray for us.

The nine principal vices to which Man is subject
are these: tristia, philargyria, fornicatio, superbia,
cenodoxia, gastrimargia, acedia, ira, and tædium cordis.

Midnight. I awake in a city of metallic birds
turning on their standards with every breeze. Who knows
the significance of this ?

The future is hidden from all save God,
but at the same time we should bear in mind
that the intelligence of angels, however fallen,
may be acute. In shrewdness and sibylline perspicuity
they excel Mankind, and proceed into the future
by means of logical deduction.

Ethnographies and topographies shall perish;
the world draws near its anargonic revolution.

I wear the lining of miniver fur
which I, a physician, am privileged to wear.

From my belt dangles my sword
and my jacket is covered with dust
as I enter the gates of Ingolstadt
preceded by fame and the accusations of Donne.
To every corner of the earth have I been
and am not yet finished with travel.
From Croatia to Walachia will I seek the truth.
And if I find it not there
then will I go at night to Brandenburg
or Transylvania. Have I drawn wine from dry wood?
Does a black poodle trot by my side ?

Dawn. I arise from the sand of a beach
wearing a mysterious ring.
I see a bone and the wing of a dove
that has drowned.
I feel I have been here many ages,
joined to the annelid
and mollusc. This meaning is distinct,
yet will pass unnoticed by most.

My brother knows of an island of red pearls
where a pearl is placed in the mouth of the dead
and pepper is white. It is far away,
but when the wind comes out of the west we will go;
the earth may roll on its axis before we return,
if ever we do.

Galileo died in captivity
the year Newton was born. For their sake
I continue.

As soon as it had been demonstrated that there were
mountains and valleys on the surface of the moon
those who believed celestial bodies must be faultless

argued that these irregularities were not real
but merely apparent, and the moon must be enclosed
by a vitreous substance invisible to Mankind.

Miguel Servete discovered the circulation of the blood and
published *De Trinitatis Erroribus*, among other things,
for which he was burnt.

Descartes was preparing to issue his pamphlet on the
nature of the universe when he was informed of the fate
of Galileo, which is the reason he locked up his thesis
in a desk. It was not published until fourteen years
after his death.

I am like a deaf mute with a message
of the utmost importance
addressing someone ignorant of my fantastic language,
who must resort to a frightful pantomime
of sighs and gestures.
Laboriously, I am transcribing reality.

The Eskimo has twenty words
to express the conditions of snow.
The Tokelau Islander
has nine words for the ripeness of coconut.
I have not one word
to express my longing.

Da amantem et sentit quod dico; only another lover,
with love like mine, could understand.

According to Sir Thomas Browne
there is something of divinity in us
that was before the elements
and does not owe homage to the sun.

He believes we are in the image of God,
and whosoever does not understand this
cannot ever learn the Alphabet of Man.

Those wondrous and magical reflections
which have been set down in *Urne-Burial*
were undertaken following the discovery of
ancient sepulchral urns at Norfolk.
This is the reason I will go
and dig and sift my father's ashes,
to find and write out our mutual meanings.

Tat tuam asi; thou also.

There is a wind which blows in August across the Ægean.
It is called Meltem and will carry us from the Cyclades
to Alexandria.

The spiral, the fish, the sea-fan
and the anchor—all are mystic symbols.

I have just this moment learned
the *Argonaut* is sunk in the Yellow Sea!
My brother was aboard
using another man's name.
He was older than I
and never told me what he sought.
I remember when he was a boy
he one day scooped up a handful of mud
and flung it across a white swan
floating on the water on an English lake.
And never once the swan looked at him
but dived; and in a moment
we both saw it rise again, shining and pure.

What shall I say next?

I will speak of treasure hoards
and of women, who hate and fear the sea,
who become excited by the presence of coral
and never tire of gathering it,
and lock its branches in their jewel cases,
which seldom are open to display.

I shall describe how the sun seethes with unconscionable
fury, how polar snows melt and boil, dry winds
rage across the globe and fantastic patterns of celestial
flame soar over crumbled mountains. Oceans wrinkle
to smoldering, bubbling pits. These matters I expect;
these we should anticipate.

I affirm that I have seen the Unicorn
and learned of dromedaries beyond the river
where once I bathed; and assert my belief
the realm of the Khan is not far.

I have contemplated three kingdoms
which are called Marata, Acus, and Totonteac,
because I know the way. I beg you to accompany me
in search of them. If you believe
I will not ever find them
you will not hesitate to go. But if I do
and we should enter into Totonteac
to the sound of native flutes—into a city
alive with parrots, bright with shells
and topaz pendants—tell me, if you know,
how should we stay, or ever quite return?

Nor is this all.

I remind you that in Peru
are ageless Inca walls
so narrowly fitted
that the blade of a knife
cannot slide between two stones.

I will allow you to discover what I mean;
knowledge is subject to long interpretation.
We have much that we were never given.

Nostradamus informs us that there exist
certain persons to whom almighty God reveals
by impressions formed upon their understanding
secrets of the future, according to judicial astrology,
as happened in previous times when men were possessed
by powers and voluntary faculties, as if by fire.

In a Portuguese castle stands a gigantic brazen head.
Those who consult it are told whatever they require,
whether this concerns what is past, what is, or
what remains to be. None but fools ignore fatidic words.

Last night I dreamt of an object
gilded and embossed
with cryptic insignia. Birds
circled anxiously above it,
cawing and screaming.
I watched them pretend to pluck out
its single eye, but tilt and stream away
with cries of desperate anguish.
And I understood it must be
toward the use of this
we labor. There is no doubt;
where the heart leads, we follow.
But still, like horrified birds

not one of us presumes
to touch the regnant evil.

According to Zosimus the panopolitan
we that look into a mirror
look not at shadows, but at what these shadows hint,
understanding reality through fictive appearance.

On the 10th day of February
in the year 1896
an explosion took place in the sky
above Madrid. People rushed from their houses
praying and shrieking, and
gazing up, beheld a luminous cloud filled with debris.
For a period of five hours the streets of Madrid
were bombarded with stones!

In Salzburg there is an iron cube
shaped by artificial means. Four sides are neatly faced,
the other two being convex, and around it
runs a geometrically contrived groove.
On a table beside this thing
lies the lump of coal in which it was found.

Let us doubt without unbelief of things
to be believed.
This is the voice of Augustine.

Time will be.
Time is.
Eleven hours have passed.
These are vatic words.

The cattle shall be stricken with murrain,
ulcers plague Everyman! Frogs, flies,

and mosquitos shall besiege the nation! Hail destroy
each crop, locusts absorb the remnant! Darkness
settles at noon.

During the last days of the Plague
a goose girl from Przytullen was seen
capering among the bodies, adorned
with jewels stolen from the dead. Mindless
in the solitude of vacant halls she played,
a baroness between indifferent shadows.

It is late. The moon is obscured by ragged clouds.

Troops poise at the border; they await
their benediction.

We are cautioned by the venerable Duns Scotus,
Doctor Subtilis, to distinguish between volition
which is efficacious and the volition of complaisance.

If it is true, as the Gnostics claim, we are devoid of
will, then Evil is not a consequence of voluntary
transgression, but emanates from the Creator. Therefore
God is a malignant power, Lord of the Kingdom of Darkness.

With all my heart and most unfeignedly
and with all my will and most deliberately
do I wholly renounce God, Father, Son,
and Holy Ghost; the most Holy Mother of God;
each Angel, and that who has guarded me;
the Passion of Our Lord, Jesus Christ,
His blood and all its merits,
and my lot in Paradise, and all prayers
that are made or may be offered for me.

Full of doubt, hesitantly, I approach my truth.
Centuries are required to create a flower.

Marmotius in his chronicle records how farmers dared not
observe the rising sun, and sailors would not look at the
sea, for fear they should be called Mithraists. This has
its parallel in our day.

The principle of regicide was first espoused
by the Popes of Rome.

The father of Christ was a Roman soldier named Panthera.

The Artotyritæ, for adding cheese to the bread,
were declared heretic and vigorously persecuted.

I have heard that those who cannot participate
in other lives are those who live most in fear of Death.
If this is true, let it be.

Light of our darksome journey here, with days
dividing night from . . .

Once my brother told me with great bitterness
his dream of children dancing on the tumulus
and of how, when he awoke, his pockets—
which he had thought were stuffed with gold doubloons—
were empty; and he held a few dusty pebbles in his hand.

I believe in the value of gold, which is
sunlight petrified by the activities of time.

I recognize that whoever sets out in search of treasure,
from the Magistri to Father Pacifique, must follow

in the footsteps of some other.

Now the rain has stopped. The clouds
half are lifting. I am young, there will be
time enough. I will devote these moments
to leisure, to the arrangement of my plans.

It is claimed he will locate the treasure of Sijilmassa
who is able to point out the mouth of the river Ziz,
which sinks in the desert sand. Innumerable years
shall have passed and long been forgotten when I come
to the end of this.

Gruet,
having written the word *Nonsense!*
in Calvin's book,
was executed for blasphemy
and treason.

Perhaps it is true, we live merely on the verge of
a Christian era. The stones we noticed
were burnt, and fragments of human skin floated
in the river, down the estuary toward the Inland Sea.
Today, when obscurities baffle learned men,
what interpretation should be considered certain?

I come now to consider seven bishops of Portugal
who stood together on the deck of a caravel
when a white albatross was observed to fly over.
This I take to mean that somewhere in the Indian Islands
the Seven Cities of Antilia will be found!

I do not know if I am awake or dreaming.
There is a metallic taste in my mouth
as though I had swallowed a coin.

Beads of moisture appear on my skin.
My fingers tremble. The evening is cool,
yet I feel warm. I behold
marvelous figures turn languorously
among trees whose limbs are writhing tentacles.
On the wall a circular Peruvian rug
is pulsing with universal regularity—
I lean toward a new existence.

Mirabile visu!

The great astrologer and cosmographer Toscanelli
assures me that a voyage of five thousand miles
due west will bring me to Quinsay, a city of China
which is praised by Marco Polo. I have no reason
to doubt him, but still I am uneasy. I have sailed
a hundred leagues beyond the island of Tile
and have measured the latitude, which I found
to be 73°, not 63°, as I had been informed.
Nor does it lie on the meridian where Ptolemy
swore the West began, but lies much further.
Therefore I am uneasy. I wonder if I shall live
to taste the sweet barbaric fruits of Quinsay.

All is possible to those who believe.

Like the annular rings of a tree
prophetic dreams increase.

I am depressed and restless, full of a strange doubt.
I have lain here all day among the pines, face down,
listening to the sough of the wind. Easter is near,
familiar mysteries evoke no respect; I have traveled
too far.

Estevan! Estevan!
Ay, thou Moor!
Where lies this fabled city?
I,
Francisco Vásquez de Coronado,
am come to claim thee with all thy riches
in the name of His Excellence,
Nuño de Guzmán, Viceroy of New Spain.
Mother of Christ, where does this desert end?
Ay, Mother of Christ . . .

Why should I feel as desolate as I do?
Is it that I am sick of travel and I am sick
and far away, and swiftly night comes on?

Whatever I imagine,
or that I apperceive,
does not exist
separate from me.

My brother lay on his back and his eyes were open.
His expression was very calm and wise.
I had searched all day, and when I found him
I unfolded my arms as though I were a bird
and thus did I float above him,
gazing earnestly into his face.
His hair streamed in the green current of the Gulf,
bright fish hovered against his fingertips.
He never spoke, nor moved, nor cared
that I had looked for him so long; nor that I
could not bear to see him as he used to be.

Pass by that which you do not love.

Twice I traveled the Orinoco in search of Manoa,
but yet I could not discover it. Next
I sought the Straits of Annian; I heard of someone
who had broached the gap and would tell me
where to turn, if only I could speak to him.
Now I prepare for a longer journey
that will lead me to far greater wealth—
greater than the temple of Daibaba
or the fabulous palace of Cubanacan!
I go in search of Norembega,
which has been called a shadow and a dream.

It is well known how the early cartographers were vain,
and to fortify their reputations would delineate
not only what was known and what had been reported
but also many coastlines, mountains, rivers
and settlements which did not exist. Among these men
was one by the name of Clavus, who was distinguished
from his colleagues by his feeling for humor;
and where they called their fictitious villages
by whatever name occurred to them, Clavus
on his map of the Greenland coast gave to his points
the words of a Danish song, which are these,
commencing high on the eastern coast and reading
downward to the southern extremity, and upward
toward the west:
There lives a man by a Greenland bourn
And Spjellebod he is named.
More he has of a lousy hide
Than he has of bacon fat.
Northward drifts the sand.

We took on board two Gælic slaves
who were called Haki and Hekja,

this latter being a woman.
And the King said they could outrun a deer.
And we put them ashore past Furdustrandir
and told them to run as far as they could
and return in three days.
What the King said was true.
They wore a strange hooded garment
open at the sides and without sleeves,
fastened between the legs with a button and a loop.
They understood what we told them and ran
among the rocks with the speed of a deer.
Three days passed. We saw them
run toward us. The man carried
an ear of wild wheat. The woman bore
a bunch of grapes. We took them back on board
and continued our journey.
I willingly would be a Gælic slave
to see where the wild wheat grows.

Palm, fern, and breadfruit
where we remembered snow
we found near Svalberd,
we have traveled so far.

Let the heron fly with long strokes.
Let the horns beat against every height.
On my wrist I carry the Iceland falcon.
O beautiful!
Beautiful in the morning light!

I will pause
and begin again.

The savage told us he knew of a mysterious site
where we might find what we were looking for.

We questioned him as to how old it might be,
but he could answer only that it was very old;
not even his grandfather, whom he remembered,
could think of anyone who knew when this place
had been inhabited. For that reason we went there
one winter morning. The day was bitter cold
and it seemed to us we would have been wiser
to have stayed at home. Across a stony hill
the Eskimo led us; we came at last to the place
he commended. And there we began to dig
the frozen ground, hopeful our efforts might yield
a runic stone or a bronze church bell, such as we
had unearthed before. That day and the next
we made little progress, nor for three days after.
Yet we were not dissuaded, since we believed
some object of high importance had been laid
in nearby ground. We thought it was a corpse
just below; and then someone sighed, holding
his breath, and we knew we had not been mistaken.
We looked to see. Bundles as hard as any stone!
Five wood crosses and five bodies wrapped
in medieval garments, frozen six centuries,
we found that day. And we who looked on those
serene and yellowed faces, cool as carved features
of ivory chess pieces, who clasped, each to its breast
a white wood cross—three men, a woman, and a child—
knew that they, even as we, could not but dread
the imminent loss of Heaven.

Languages of medieval Europe had no word to express
the concept of civilization.

The hands of the clock are turning.
Darkness gathers. Overhead, the wheeling falcon waits.
Eleven hours are past. *Sanctificetur nomen tuum* . . .

Is it so, as I have heard, that each nation
the same as Everyman, conceals within itself
diabolic forces awaiting the chosen moment?

Toward future ages fall adumbrations of the holocaust;
meticulous horrors sing a pure Euclidean song.

It has been calculated
that Mankind is eighteen days of age,
basing this on the assumption that Man has existed for
one million years,
and the earth may be habitable two billion more.
An infant that is eighteen days old
will cry when it is hungry or in pain,
and is able to follow a bright light with its eyes.

Now is the time for a dreamer.

Yesterday I found a strange coin among hundreds
in a bronze bowl at the marketplace in Damascus.
Unerringly my fingers picked it out; it was
elliptical and had no date. On one side
loomed a gynandrous head with classic features
beneath the word *Creation*. On the obverse
a male figure was seated, with a spear, or staff
in his left hand. On the palm of his right hand
a smaller figure stood, but whether this was meant
to be an infant or a woman I could not decide.
The inscription was not legible, yet I am sure
it would tell of cruelty, œstrum, cacoëthes,
depravity and malevolence, and every degradation.

Cecco d'Ascoli, for suggesting the earth might be
a sphere, was burnt alive.
Giordano Bruno, holding that the universe evolved,

was burnt alive.
Antonio de Dominis wrote on the nature of light.
After death his body was exhumed
and formally burnt.
Cernit omnia Deus vindex.

Tomorrow we will believe, if not today.

There is a city called Luz where the Angel of Death
has no power, until those that live within its walls
have discovered what lies without.

Several days we spent among the ruins,
reputed to be the oldest on the continent.
We found numerous disks of silver and copper,
brooches, pottery, tiaras, bones, quantities
of gold filigree, and a few ornamental beads.
We found also the carving of a hideous deity
flanked by fifty-two figures, each in the likeness
of a winged man. There was a tiger of solid gold
and some lesser animals, and a sacrificial stone
hollowed in the center, with a groove to accommodate
the neck. The lake, we were told, has receded
during the centuries. It now lies nine leagues
from the temple. Today the surrounding fields
are cultivated; dolmens and fallen lintels
are found in yellow barley stubble.

According to Albertus Magnus, our descent owes less to our
search for pleasures than to the fallacy of our reason.

Perseus, when he had rid the world of the Gorgon
and set down the bleeding head on the sandy shore,
washed his fingers in the sea. And it is said
coral sprang out of this blood where it ran in the water.

Here is a magic emblem, the symbol of our race.

Again today, prescience and afterknowledge;
I have no further doubt.
We are void of soul; we are not immortal; we will not
endure, nor prevail.

Saint Epiphanius, having detailed
the abominations of the Gnostics, concludes:
Why should I not speak of things you do not fear to do?
By speaking thus, I hope to fill you with horror
of the turpitudes you commit.

Mid-afternoon.
A cluster of metal objects
has been uncovered
on the coastal dunes
ringed by a chill sea-wind.
They are aimed at the north
and no birds reel overhead.
Natural things look upon us
and our wonders with repugnance.

As our grasp on reality progressively weakens
and the content of our mind becomes ever more primitive,
chaotic, and bewildered, we may assume and maintain
postures symbolic of our inner strain
while we seek to convey incommunicable feelings or ideas
through fantastic gestures.

It seems to me we are gathering in a cellar
for some obscure but malignant purpose. By candlelight
I perceive a ragged priest turning the pages of a book
whose cover is hairy, made out of the pelt of a wolf.
The leaves of this book are crimson. The priest

mumbles and mutters through clenched teeth; and
suddenly I observe him elevate the black Host,
which is filthy with writhing maggots, and a chalice
of cracked pewter. Adorning his chasuble
is a broken cross, smeared with human excrement.

Rotten posts are painted; gilded nuts
taste dry.
In secrecy we bear a lie.

*He is nowhere upon the mountain where we had thought
to find Him, nor among galactic systems.*

The depression I felt since yesterday has gone. I
will sit up tonight, until dawn, to meditate.
I feel strangely sensate, and wakeful.
My life is not half so worthless as I had imagined.
I shall not decay, I shall not give myself over to worms.
I shall not witness corruption within my heart.
I shall have my being, I shall live and germinate;
and I shall wake up in peace. The shape of my vision
endures, after the form of my countenance is taken.

This pallid flower, which appears utterly motionless,
is growing. I have measured its petals
with a compass: I am close to the perception of miracles.
Delicately I hold this flower, as though I were
a subtle portrait of my self which is painted
by the German who calls himself Albrecht Dürer.

There is a black stain in Wartburg castle
where Martin Luther flung his inkhorn at the Devil.

Melanchthon speaks of one Johannes Faustus who was born
at Knütlingen, in Württemberg, not far from his own home,

who studied magic in Cracow, and afterwards traveled
and talked of mysterious things. My brother, when I
told him this, inquired if I were by singular coincidence
that same Faustus, because of my chthonic journey
and because he could not understand me. I am able
to see him now, where he stood, frightened by my laughter.

That which is common to the working of disordered minds
may be approximate to the writings of our vatic poets.
We do not know, as yet, whether this is through
some accident, or by intent. We should be hopeful
it is for a purpose, in which case we surmise
our poets have grown angry with us, but still are sane.
If they, however, do not recognize their end,
it must follow they have gone insane. And from this
follows an inescapable, horrifying implication.

I can no longer say whether I am dreaming
in a world awake, or if it may be our world
that lies asleep, and I alone am conscious.

A voice has said he is held prisoner by the Turks
in a narrow cave on the mountainside.
His clothing is in rags. He does not eat or sleep.
No matter in what language he is questioned,
the answer comes back in Aramaic
that he is Cartaphilus, who asked of Jesus,
Why dost thou linger here?

The year is turning as a leaf turns in its season, as
the earth turns, as the life of Man.

Beneath the first pillar on the left,
in the Great Mosque of Cordova, the Arab

Ibn Röchd has buried a ray of sunlight.

Nothing escapes my notice
save the passage of time.

I am told of a lamp replenishing itself while it burns,
which for eight centuries has illuminated the crypt of
Christian Rosenkreutz, for whose body we search in vain.

The alchemist Auriger observes that nothing shall be born
to a better state unless it first has died and undergone
the dissolution and putrefaction of previous principles.

No malady is subject to cure, say the astrologers,
for sickness betokens the outcome of original sin.

The death of Canches at Orleans
represents the dissolution of matter.

In Egypt
every manner of serpent and dragon
was painted circular, the head swallowing
its tail, to signify
they had come from one and the same; and that this
sufficed unto itself, and this form
and this motion
became its own perfection.

I do not think too highly of men; nor too lowly.

Peter the Hermit preached the order
thoroughly, communicating his madness
until Europe surged and boiled.
Unius dementia dementes efficit multos.

Always we discover at the heart of tragedy
a core of silence.

We know of Saint Dionysius
that when his head had been chopped from his body
he picked it up and carried it;
and walked to the place where he wanted to be buried.
To what prayer will you listen, if not to this?

There are means by which we one day will achieve
the liberation of Man, his deliverance and salvation,
the transmutation of base instinct
into the precious metal of his constitution.
On that day shall illusion become reality.

King Wenceslaus demanded of John Nepomucene
that he reveal the confession of the King's
wife, Joan. This the priest refused to do,
which is the reason he was seized and bound,
dragged through the streets of Prague, and
flung into the turbulent Moldau. This is why
we have preserved the tongue of a priest,
why it remains whole, and retains the color,
the size, and the strength of a living tongue.

God forgive
this life,
monstrous
and filled
with iniquity.

According to Cardinal Lepicier
the characteristics of a miracle are these:
It shall occur with relative infrequency,

since God did not create the world
in order to interfere continually with His own laws.
Since it is of divine origin, the event should be
reasonable, and of moral character,
not a fantasy or prodigy of dubious merit.
There is always some evident spiritual motivation.
It procures the general or individual welfare.
It is most frequently instantaneous,
although it may be progressive in its unfolding.
Its effects should be persistent,
but this condition is not indispensable.
Because of their very nature
certain miracles are limited in time.
Ordinarily it shall occur in answer to prayer.

Is this what they have brought me, being hungry,
the Sun and the Moon?

There is known to be a figure which we call our Savior
or our Redeemer, that lies half-asleep in the mind of Man,
waking each time we are committed to a grievous error.

Seven Christians of Ephesus
who lived under the reign of the Emperor Decius
fled from the city and fell asleep in a cave
on Mount Celion. When they wakened one said to Malchus,
who was their leader :
Go to the city and buy bread for us
and discover, if you can, what Decius means to do.
Then Malchus went into the city and was puzzled
that everything was strange,
and the baker from whom he bought bread
looked in astonishment at the coins he proffered
and would not take them, saying:

Tell me, how should I spend coins
that date from the reign of Decius?
I believe we are like those seven Christians of Ephesus
that fled their persecution
and fell asleep in a cave on Mount Celion.

In the core of an oak Merlin sleeps fitfully—
deep, deep in the forest of Broceliande.

In the heart of a mountain Charlemagne dreams;
crowned and armed, he waits the hour
when he shall deliver the Franks out of bondage.

John the Divine dreams in his grave. The ground is shaken
over his breast with every breath he draws. He awaits
the Antichrist, against whom he shall bear witness
during the days that precede the Second Coming.

Joseph of Arimathea sleeps in the city of Sarras.

As crystal from fluid precipitates,
my thought resolves.
I am Magus. Trust in me.

I am able to discourse with great learning
upon projections, cimentations, sublimations, elixirs
of life, and the universal alkahest.
To everyone I boast thoroughly of my intercourse
with salamanders and sylphs,
and of my power to draw diamonds out of the earth
by incantation, and by the magic of my song!
Often they ask why I spend my life
in search of phantoms, as they are pleased to say.
I reply that not this life or moment do I count,
but these thousand more, until I transmute

the fabulous stone, which some believe is no other
than the Grail—since that can be no phantom
or unworthy fragment thrown from the brain of a man,
as though his soul were a spinning wheel!

Late one December afternoon we encountered him
in the wintry lemon light beside the athanor,
wearing a greatcoat and fur bonnet.
Above his head, dangling from the ceiling, was the pelt
of a dog. Formulæ covered the walls.
Culpels, flasks, retorts, alembics, porcelain crucibles,
pots of orpiment and electuary . . .

Appearance passes;
truth abides.

We stand as the terminal symbol.

In Assyria a mountain has burst
and a Greek scroll been revealed,
proclaiming the end of the world.

Certain excavations have brought to light
ten thousand inscriptions in the Etruscan language,
of which fully eight thousand are sepulchral!

We know that from a distance it is impossible for Man
to distinguish Christ from Antichrist, whose face
seldom is monstrous or evil.

Saint Vincent Ferrer has allowed the world as many years
as there are verses to the Psalms, which number 2537.

Shall the visions of the heart be troubled by discretion?

I have talked with a certain priest
that gained access to a convent of nuns
and left them believing he was the Vicar of Christ
and they become His brides, belonging to him,
who vows wild figs were never so sweet.

On the central panel of a medieval triptych
somewhere in Europe stands the figure
of a woman from whose vulva
radiates a profusion of luminous xanthic lines
resembling the spokes of a wheel!
A child who paints the midday sun will
imagine such lines in order to represent
the inconceivable power of the object.

I awake
congested with desire.
There is blood on my hands;
I have lived celibate so long.

The *Rituale Romanum* is highly instructive.
When a woman is to be exorcised
the priest is advised to have responsible persons
hold on to her tightly
while her body is agitated by the demon.
He is advised to show care
that he inspire obscene thoughts
neither in himself nor in others.

Bodin, a notable jurist of the Middle Ages, observes
that women are peculiarly liable to sorcery
and witchcraft, being liars, having larger intestines
than men, and being constituted, as they are,
halfway between man and beast.

There was an age when a woman who loved her husband
would sheathe her body with wild honey
and roll herself on a bed of corn, and make of this
a cake meant only for her husband to eat. Of
conquered repugnance are ultimate pleasures born;
paths that lead into a forest may not lead out again.

The magic cake of antiquity was known as the *confarreatio*.
Across the woman's naked thighs a board was placed
and on this board was set a small oven. A fire
was lighted, and the hotly seasoned cake thus impregnated
with her pain—and the ripe, burnt flesh of love.
Lovers eating this grow blind to other women.

We know our word for love is derived from the Sanskrit
lubhyati, implying desire.

Women discover their husband by the quiet, obstinate wish
that works magically, like the fixed stare of a Serpent.

I have read in the Bestiary that if a virgin
shall be taken into the woods and seated on a hillock,
a Unicorn will be attracted to her and will come
and kneel down and lay his head in her lap.

Lions, when they are ill, seek Monkeys to eat.
Yet animals forget naturally what they have done,
and the cruelty they practice does not well up in them
as it does in us. We should like to forget our sins,
but we are unable not to remember.

I have learned that I shall be always what I am.

The Sien-seng are men of extreme continence,

leading lives of unbelievable austerity. They eat bran
which has no flavor, and do not take a wife.
Their chins and their heads are shaven,
and they wear robes of blue sacking.
They sleep on mats made of harsh wicker, and worship fire,
and keep idols toward which they prostrate themselves.
The form of each idol is female, and each is given
a female name, which is why the Sien-seng cry out
in anguish, repeatedly, the names of many women.

I have talked with a man who had himself immured,
leaving only one window through which he was handed
a bowl of lentil, which he befouled before he ate,
and denied himself its final seed, and prayed
and excoriated himself. In the seventh month
a woman appeared to him, kneeling over him,
and through a perforation in her belly he looked out
upon a desert. To all who questioned him, he replied
that vinegar is sweeter than the taste of pucelage.

Suffering is of itself neither good nor evil.

The river creates its course and the banks
which contain it, and no two are identical.

I hate and dread each day, I have lain here
so long, helpless and tormented. Once again it is
dawn. I stare at the wall, seeing the print of Arashiyama
gather colors from darkness.

According to Locke, the Englishman, if I shall trace
the progress of my thoughts, observing
with close attention how they repeat and add
themselves to each other, uniting the simplest receipts
of sensation or reflection, I shall find myself

traveled further than I would have imagined.
By comparison, there are aborigines in the Bay of Bengal
who have not yet learned a method for making fire.

At Harappa, in the Montgomery district of the Punjab,
has been found evidence of a civilization
that hitherto was unknown. Eight hundred archival seals
made of stone and copper have been recovered,
each containing, on the average, half a dozen glyphs.
But as to the people who made and used these vouchers
nothing whatsoever is recorded—their race,
the names of their kings, or their language.

I have been watching the cartographer
who is at work on a map, bent over it with dividers
and similar contrivances of which I have little knowledge.
The longitudes and latitudes are meaningless,
nor do I recognize the outline of any coast,
so foreign it is. I have inquired
concerning what terrain this might be,
but got back no answer except the crackle of parchment.
I have reason to believe he is obsessed by us
and endeavors to describe the boundaries of our estate.

Someone has said that on the 15th day of August
a boy in a Japanese city deliberately burned to ashes
the one thing that had not been taken from him,
which was a schoolbook he found while sifting the ruins
of his father's home. In this book were several poems,
and exercises in the art of reading. No one thus far
has explained his act. But is it not clear to everyone?
The boy had perceived the absurdity of such things.

Lord Macaulay informs us how democratic institutions
in due course shall obliterate liberty and civilization.

Ora pro nobis.
Pray for us.

I spoke to a woman
who said that a few moments after noon
the buildings of the city
suddenly were illuminated, black
and crenulate as medieval watchtowers.
Two nations' prodigious error
bloomed and softly shut like petals
within a bleak Ægean dream.

It has been reported that the first troops
to enter the area
were cheerful to the point of
euphoria, pausing frequently
to distribute sweets
and to play with the children.

I have heard that in Landsberg prison
south of Munich
fifteen enemy officers waited under sentence of death
for crimes against humanity
until, owing to circumstances
which were considered beyond control,
they were allied with their captors;
whereupon their sentences were commuted to imprisonment
with the provision of early parole
in order that they might be recommissioned.
Singular skills are useful.

The blows from their rubber truncheons
sounded monotonously, it is said,
like the plunging of animal hooves
through a muddy field.

Brief is our pain.

Die Kunst ist lang
und kurz ist unser Leben.

Christmas Day.

The horizon is obscured;
a north wind blows.

The sky is lowering and sullen, whiter than paste
that children use; our compass drifts unnaturally
as though in portent of things to come.

It is rumored that somewhere in the Canadian arctic
lies a valley warmed by geysers and hot springs,
where the climate is tropical and serpents flourish,
and fabulous monsters roam undisturbed by the passage
of ages. If this is true, then all that seems most real
about us is but the thinnest substance of a dream.

Magister Adam has written that beyond Wineland
no habitable place is found in the ocean.
The land is filled with intolerable ice
and utter darkness. Prince Harald, exploring
to the full breadth of the North Ocean,
scarcely escaped with safety the gulf of an abyss
when the bounds of the earth grew misty and dark
before his eyes.

Last night an albatross flew over.
Metallic is the moon and cold
on the slope of ominous telluric waves.
Where we are headed I know not,
nor have courage to inquire.

Lat. 46.23 N.; Long. 160.10 E.
I am chilled and sick at heart.

We have come so far north
God knows if we will see
this winter's end, or
once more behold a tree.
The falcon's knuckles
have frozen to his prey
and one island of ice
encloses us. The wood
that makes our boat is
frozen as hard as a bone.
We cannot guess if this be
day or night, nor upon
which continent we are bound
nor why, but that it were
madness to linger here.

Symbols adumbrate the end.

We buried him at the foot of a vein of white quartz
standing like a monument, so that when the savages
were gone away we might return and find his corpse
and carry this with us back to his children. But
the way is long and full of danger. We are counseled
and told it would be unwise, and certain we should
lose our lives together in this land. Down to rock
we dug his grave and in it placed him hurriedly.
And on his left side was placed his sword. On his
right the axe. Laid over him the great shield. And
his head was to the West so that he faces the dawn
from whence comes the Lord of the Resurrection Morning.
And then we departed.

I know now that things are not what they seem.

By cold batrachian jellies are we linked
to blinded fluid things
that seep and writhe through ageless protoplasmic floors.

Only a moment has passed;
I am like a beaker of liquid subtly altered
by a single drop of foreign essence.

This is the 12th day of June. The water
has risen, strangely black and vitreous,
and fantastic reptiles we thought long preterlapsed
appear on every side, though I alone can see them.
Thus, I have asked myself if they exist;
since if they do not, nor ever have, then I am mad.
I see them plainly, as I am able to perceive
our future course through remote and secular channels.

It has just been reported from Cape Artemision that
in a net belonging to a fisherman
an immense object was caught;
but as it was being hauled to the surface
the net broke under its weight,
and the unknown thing settled quickly out of sight.
There is much we know in regard to corporeal objects,
but less in regard to the human mind, and still less
of our beginnings.

I will now consider more exactly,
and with extreme probity,
whether I am able to discover within myself
further intimations
that shall burgeon richly. Nothing
must obstruct these meditations.

I have been thinking of my uncle
who was gone twenty years,
and brought home a sea chest filled with Eastern brocade,
jewels in a leather pouch, perfumes, and exquisite books
illuminated by hand in lavish colors
with gold facings; who spoke of marvels he had seen
and of oil paintings,
and dishes he had tasted, and of strange
musical instruments. While at his feet
with neither a word nor any smile,
her black eyes brilliantly fixed on his face
and copper bells attached to her ankles,
lounged a Semitic dancer, whose name he never told us.
Thus always do we seek our own delight.

Certain peoples abstain from blood,
the flesh of swine, and all things strangled;
and in their lamentation they employ these words:
Jeru! Jeru! Masco! Salem!
by which we think they recall Damascus
and Jerusalem.

In Syria is the river Sabbatius,
so named because its rivers flow toward the sea
six days of the week; but on the seventh day
its waters come to a stop.

Except for the miracles of revelation as narrated
in the Old and in the New Testaments
we are at liberty to doubt, or to believe.

For beatification two miracles are required;
for martyrdom, none.

It is in the diary of Albrecht Dürer
that we read of the slaughtered ones
which lie across God's altar
and cry for vengeance;
and of how the voice of God replies, saying
they shall wait
until an accomplished number of innocents are dead,
when justice may be done.

Perhaps it is true,
we are like those doves that stand
between cathedral bells
until they have lost all sense of hearing.

I know what I cannot prove, by reason or experiment.

Eppur si muove.

I divide the world into these parts:
that which is pleasing to me I say is choice
or natural; but that toward which I am averse
I say is repugnant to all Mankind.

A warm breeze from the mountain
does little to assuage my illness;
I am nervous and excited; I am restive
and pluck at the fringe of my blanket.
Soon there will be a visitor I dread.

Someone has knocked at the door!
I will not respond. My candle bends to a fitful wind;
what is seen is made of things which seldom appear.

Who can hear me ? Where should I turn?
Actus non facit reum nisi mense sit rea.

I think what I remember with the utmost clarity
is not the actual circumstance of his death,
although I had noticed how the bullets struck him,
had seen him gaze beyond the attentive soldiers
and then, half-knowingly, throw himself backward
against the rocks. Blood trickling from his nostrils
failed to disturb me, nor blood appearing—
magically, some exclaimed—through his open lips.
What astonished me was that a strange woman should
rush forward to embrace him, as if he were a living man.

We read in the Bible that there shall be a time
when many that sleep in the earth shall awake,
some to everlasting life.

Rosh-ha-Shannah. A few minutes after five this morning
was seen a great comet with a curving trail of fire.
It ascended and all day hung blazing, undiminished and
malevolent. Fishes leapt out of the river, dogs howled,
houses swayed. Apparitions such as this provide warning;
they serve to remind us we cannot live materially.

One whose name I never learned
has come this way.

It is claimed that by his work each man celebrates
the psychic structure of his life.

I have spoken with a Philosopher who postulates
that nothing whatsoever is mandatory,
the opposite of which is conceivable! If this is true,
how can I be obligated to any man?

I have made the acquaintance of a Tactician who
calculates that, should the Senator's argument

be accepted, less than one of eighty thousand shall
survive. It is my hope that of these few
the Senator may be one. I conceive of no retribution
one-twentieth so just.

I could distinguish boats in the harbor below. It was
late afternoon when I flew over. I could visualize
those men preparing to quit work. I could imagine myself
in their position—I, too, have a wife. It was not that
I eagerly did what you know I have done; it was,
to put the matter in the simplest terms, a function.
Do you understand? I was merely handed my orders.
In fact, I never had seen the young man who approached,
saluted, and gave me the envelope I was expecting.
What should I have done but accept? Should I have
woodenly remained where I was, protesting to superiors . . .

Toward evening the gates of Heaven are shut
and no prayer obtains admission.

In the library at Upsala is preserved the contract
by which Daniel Salthenius sold himself to the Devil.

Since noon I have been contemplating
the Lord Chancellor of the Realm, Sir Thomas More,
who steadfastly rejected each petition
of the King of England; who therefore was beheaded
and his head lodged upon a pole on London Bridge. Who
among us cares to reflect on this?

None dies
but has desired it.

Each part of my body knows what it is and what it does,
and lives as it will. Yet not one of us can explain

what compels us to reveal ourselves through symbols.

Duns Scotus, Doctor Subtilis, tells us
that reason cannot comprehend ideas of immortality.
Has he said who keeps the grain in storage
till it rots?

Some believe there is an icy wind steadily blowing
without remission toward our vaults.

Boethius inquires whether we do have a free will
or if the fatal chain fastens also the motions
of our mind. Tell me, if you know, and I will answer
with the date that winter sets in Babylon.

Gold and 'acle protect us from corruption.

Wheat has grown up to the gates of the city.
An owl has flown into the garden.
All night I have listened for cathedral bells,
remembering Saint-Etienne.

A crumb of *madeleine*? I do not know its taste, nor
Sunday at Combray, water lilies on the Vivonne,
no, nor the parish church. But one day in a strange city
lying alone and far down the dim west I came upon
a wicker basket filled with miniature chocolate bottles
from Czechoslovakia, each bottle wrapped in foil;
and I knew that inside each must be a sweet drink
of some colored liquid which once I tasted
when I was a child. And it seemed I always waited
before the closed portals of that first Jerusalem rose.

The legend of the Prodigal Son, I have heard, is the story
of one who could not stand to be loved.

God set free
of Malady,
every Man.
To me, say
one word
for Suffering.

We know that many saints are in Heaven,
but cannot announce with certainty that anyone is in Hell.
Yet we do believe in the existence of Hell as utterly,
or more so, as we accept the idea of Heaven.

From Nicholas Flamel we learn of hermetic arts,
and that we albify the shadow-stricken earth.

A prodigious force is directing me; I am no more than
light reflected from a mirror, illuminating what I must.

The primordial Being which is meant to show the way
will not appear until we have summoned him into existence
through the ghastly nature of our accomplishments.

Opera illius
mea sunt; this
and other works
are mine.

Redemption sings unannounced
in polyphonic voices few have heard.

Like the annular rings of a tree,
prophetic dreams increase.

We were begun in a German forest, but shall end among
white sands.

Merchants from Crete and Phœnicia
have drawn their keels on a foreign beach.
Black ramparts of Ilium cast red shadows
over bales of merchandise and sacks of coin.
This is a parable of our recalcitrance.

Since it is understood that angular momentum
can be transferred from one body of a system to another
but cannot be destroyed; since the Earth and the Moon
are a unity; since it is known that the Moon gradually
is receding from the Earth; and because we know
the curiosity of Man to be insatiable; therefore,
being given these factors, it has been computed
a time will come when the month shall equal the day.
Then the night shall be long and frigid
and life must wither and die from the heat of the day.
And we who live in perpetual darkness shall journey
half around the Earth to witness our diminishing Moon,
until it rises in the west. When this occurs
our thread of life shall be broken, as the Moon itself
must shatter, being first distorted in the sky, growing
elongate and giving way to the power of its master
until it is torn in half, then into a thousand pieces
that will create a ring around us, an arch
of famous light. The Earth will be shaken by fearful
quivers, the animals will run up from the ground,
and crocodiles will bellow and run through the forest,
planetoids thunder against us, and cities be submerged
under blue water. Only the fish of the Sea will survive
and through them in time, new life may evolve.

I set down all I believe and more;
it is not for me to announce the provinces of Truth.

Should I mark more than shining hours?

They are called *silos*, because they resemble
those towers in which fodder, grain, and other foods
are stored. But there is only the windy sky
around them, broken rocks, sand, weeds,
and a few burned and blasted roots. Animals,
even the smallest, will not come near this place.
It is as though they have sensed the purpose of
these objects, and comprehend them far better than we.

There is a chain of fate that links us irrevocably
to our own destruction.

Laplace was of the opinion that a comet struck the earth
during some remote era, reducing the human population
to a few individuals who lived in a primitive state
for countless centuries, occupied by the problems of
survival, until they had lost all memory of the arts;
and not until these wants were felt did they begin again,
as if Man were but newly born.

It is said the Greeks were the first
to employ argument as a deliberate instrument
toward the realization of truth. From truths
previously established they began, and proceeded
according to the laws of human thought
until they had come to their conclusion,
which was necessarily accepted, however unwelcome.

On the linen wrappings of certain mummified remains
found near the Etrurian coast are invaluable writings
that await translation.

Quem colorem habet sapientia?

Ordinary men fulfill themselves

in the company of their fellows.

I am told of a peasant who, one morning when mists
lay across his field,
picked up a feather that had dropped from
the great horse, Pegasus; who placed the feather
in his cap and abandoned the world
for a dream.

I have heard that when the wild geese move in their season
a strange tide is raised; and long after they have gone
the fowl of the barnyard leap up frantically into the air
with shrill, desperate cries—their nut-like heads
stuffed and disordered with vestigial recollections
urging them from domestic felicity toward unremembered
chasms in the presence of another, bolder skein.

Nothing existed before me; nothing will exist after me.

Myth, art, and dreams are but emanations
from ancestral spheres.

Karma, which is the wheel of fate,
is indestructible. A new world shall be born
that it may continue to fulfill its endless process.

We are to regard the world as an empty trifle,
so said Buddha; then alone
will it yield happiness, enabling us to live blissfully
throughout life's vicissitudes.

Let us become Yasoda, the soul of woman, which calls out
to Lord Krishna in the fullness of her love, and sees
in him the universe.

As thou to me,
so I to thee.

I was greeted first on this earth by an odor of blood
and by the passionate exhalations from my mother's body,
and these I will remember longest.

It was the opinion of my father that Job's affliction
was his due; since God is just, and therefore
he who has not transgressed shall not be punished.

Some say that not Cartaphilus only, but his wife also
urged Jesus down the street. And this is why they both
are wandering, separately, and meet for a single hour
each hundred years. Always, when they meet, their moment
of reunion is embittered, thinking of years to come.

Adon-olom, asher-molach, b' terem kol . . .

In Sinai during the months of May, June, and July
beneath the tamarisk tree a substance is found
called *manna*, produced by two species of cochineal
which feed on the leaves. Each morning it is there
in the form of hyaline, aureate nuts.
This food must be gathered early, for the ants appear
to devour or carry away as much as they find.
According to our Bible, this is *manna* from Heaven.
That is from the white flowers of the tamarisk in Sinai.

Late in May, when the moon is triply ringed,
if the Wandering Jew shall chance upon two oaks
that have grown together in the form of a cross
he may sleep beneath them till the first cock crows.

The legend of the Traveler appears in every civilization,

perpetually assuming new forms, afflictions, powers,
and symbols. Through every age he walks in utter solitude
toward penance and redemption.

Nameless fears, like ancient tapestries, adorn the wall.

Primitives brought to civilization seldom are astonished
as we expect them to be; their marvels differ from ours.

A serpent will not attack a naked man
because Adam walked unharmed and unashamed in Paradise.

The blood of a goat will soften diamonds.

The crow, Cornix, can predict the future and disclose
the paths of treachery; yet it is wrong to believe
this bird understands the secrets of God.

He who is given the greatest power
is commanded to be most lenient.
This is why the King Bee,
even if he owns a sting,
does not ever make use of it.

The Honeybee, when isolated, dies of loneliness.

Natural phenomena fill me with terror.

Ominous revelations delivered by a multitude of voices
impinge upon these meditations. This morning
certain papers which belonged to my preceptor were found
on the banks of a river in Provence. I conclude
that he is gone, whereby my stature has been enhanced;
but I am afraid. I would reject this delphic obligation
if I could.

Locke has told me that if I shall add together
several units, I create the idea of a dozen; as
by the putting together of repeated ideas of various
perches, I frame that of the furlong. Similarly
I contemplate each piece of good advice.

It is said of Cabeza de Vaca that he possessed
an understanding honorable beyond that of his
contemporaries. For this he paid, wandering Jew-like
down green centuries from Bimini.
I must not neglect to account for this.

I note that the river Humber has been named
for the German, Hymyr, who ravaged the countryside
but drowned as he fled the Briton avengers.

A mysterious object just now has drifted overhead!
Fog obscured my view; still, I do not think
I would have been wise enough to describe it, except that
I suspect its course may link our world to dolmens
and stelæ.

Near the termination of its appointed life
the cooling sun will appear
from the surface of this planet, long centuries
frozen black, like a glowing violet jewel
or a luciferous droplet of blood!

Shapes of the dead stirred to Resurrection
as the gleeman sang. In time of doubt,
we confront the gnomic wisdom of our fathers.

Clouds, horses, heights, the bosom,
forbidden hungers,
solitude, gestures of enquiry and of terror,

to say nothing of revelation—
these are but a few of the many things we convey
by the use of our hand.

We learn from Hakluyt
of the ferocity of the law; of hanging
twenty at a clap,
which number appeals to our primitive sense of rhythm.

I cannot say whether I am awake, or if I sleep.

Have gone this day to see the heads of Ireton,
Bradshaw, and Cromwell, which are set up
toward the further end of the Hall. The rosebushes
are full of leaves, the ways are dusty.
It has been a strange winter, I should guess.

I have heard the sound of a goatherd's horn
across twenty miles of azure water; and
I think I will lie down to rest for a little while
in the arms of Morgan le Fay.

Perhaps I shall become not unlike those boughs
stripped of foliage and dropped into the mines of Austria,
there to become so altered, spangled, and encrusted
with salt, their nature scarcely can be determined.

Kennst du das Land wo die Citronen blühn?
Knowest thou . . .

In Scotland
an act summarily was passed
which enacted severe penalties
not merely against witches,
but toward all those who sought by any means whatever

to enter into the secrets of futurity.

I had been puzzled that my son should so engross
himself with subjects of love and
philosophy ; for these seemed more appropriate to myself.
But last night with the particular
clarity of nocturnal thought, I guessed his need
to obtain some concept
of himself in relation to the universe,
and a dim idea of where our passions bind us.

Once, I remember, I asked what he could see;
he replied there was nothing but isolate peaks
about which the water swirled and foamed.
I asked, then, what lay in the depths; he turned swiftly,
gazing at me with distress,
as though such inquiry had been born of admixture
and queer purpose. It may be, he said,
the severed arm of a giant squid, or a tree trunk
wallowing, a ribbon-fish or the corpse of a whale shark.
I listened, knowing better; for Olaus Magnus
reported the presence of this dread creature
off the coast of Scandinavia during the 16th century.
According to Magnus, it was two hundred feet in length,
with a scaly body and the mane of a horse.
Bishop Hans Egede observed it off Greenland
two centuries later—the head looming and swaying
above the waves. Now, as though in a dream
I have seen this hideous idolum
which signifies the imminent close of the Christian era.

I remember the hills of Ushita, the woods of Nigitsu.

It has been noted that after the flight of the *Enola Gay*
a fearful apathy settled on the survivors of the city;

few cared to speak, dogs seldom barked, and trees
were strangely emptied of color.

It is nearly dawn. I do not know the date.

The power of the individual is unique and unpredictable,
the slow discovery of our race.

A singular quality of intellect
cannot fail to publish itself in widening circles.
We know that al-Hallaj cried out in ecstasy
one thousand years ago: *I am the Truth! I am He!*
and for this he was tried
and cruelly tortured, and put to death.

From good must come good.
From evil,
evil.
This is karmic law.

All night I have spent observing the Heavens.
God give me to explain what I have suffered.

Our latitude is registered 12.16;
I cannot announce the hemisphere.
The moon plunges through broken clouds.
Areas of the sea
whitely illuminated
remind me of Triassic marls,
things my daughter must have seen
when she called out
through the emptiness of other nights.

We float among a vision of sea things;
I have been here countless ages.

I have heard that an amœba
drifting on the border between light and dark
turns inevitably toward the light.

The sky is pallid. There is a faint overcast;
the wind is chill. Shadows beset us.

No sight of land.

When at Panuco
the last of De Soto's men
waded ashore
an age was ending.
The bright dream of Cíbola
had fled.

Helpless are we, and miserable, bound by duties
of the flesh.

Esa es la herencia de Adán!

It may be there is no remedy
sovereign as a woman's tongue, if she
be virtuous and quiet.

Uxmal on the cool plateau, Chichen Itzá
in the jungle. A thief has stolen two gems
from the eyes of Chac Mool.

The silence is unbroken
except for the roar of a jaguar and the humming of
mosquitos. The Mayan lies asleep.
When the moon rises I will go,
for there is news of a great lake in the jungle
which they call the Lake of Paradise.

In a village beyond the river
an old man lives, who, one day when he was a youth,
went hunting and saw the glitter of it through the vines
and heard the multitude of its birds;
and since then has spent his life in wonder
that he did not choose to spend a moment on the shore.

Am I awake?

It is past eleven. I hear the nightwatch.

There is no end to those who see, or imagine
they can see, empires beyond the river.

It is known that two Franciscans traveling through Mexico
less than a century after the death of Cortés
discovered Indians worshiping the image of a horse!

We are lured by eternal cities to the north.

During the Panamanian campaign a soldier named Ojeda
amputated his own leg with a red-hot ax. This seems
to have come down to us out of the pages of Homer.

It is said they marched three full years
murdering, pillaging, and baptizing; and for their pains
found one hoard of three hundred and fifty weight
of pearls, together with a few figures carved from
iridescent shells. These shells they discarded,
divided the pearls, and went on. And it is claimed
one man grew so tired of this existence
he whirled his bag of jewels about his head,
scattering them in all directions.
But no one stooped to pick them up
or even paused, their thoughts were so fixed on home

and what should lie beyond the second hill.
Where the heart leads, we follow.

The houses, they have told us, are built of lime
and each portal sculptured of turquoise!
They assure us it cannot be much further.
I have marked on a tree the date, my name,
Ruiz, together with the name of my wife,
who is in Barcelona; that we are Christians
and I have marched this way.

When the Bible had been held aloft, which was the plan,
the savages were chopped to pieces, the women bound,
and every child past the age of nine garroted—
this age having been ascertained as the ultimate limit
beyond which redemption of the soul was not conceivable.
This, also, is relevant to our day; for we imagine
no alternative, so finite is our circumference
and regnant the plenitude of mutual apprehension.

It is our greatest bondage that through possession of
one vice, we lose the capacity for reason.

In Darien are many rich mines.

Fire on the ground is a positive sign of buried gold.

Balboa's dog received the pay of a crossbowman.

They said we should navigate that stream
whose mouth is the headwater of the Sea of Cortés,
and it might offer some approach
to El Dorado or the realm of the Khan,
where Cíbola is a part. Yet I would rather
our ships unfurled their sails to lean against white water

until we raised the coast of Spain.
There I would be content, I think, forever;
or until almonds no longer bloom in Alicante.

I do not know if I dare continue; a desire for bliss
eats ever deeper into me.

From the bay where we had come ashore
we marched in search of Cale, whose inhabitants
wear golden hats. When we could not find this place
we turned and went east, for they had told us
of a region, or a city, they call Apalachen.
And this we did find. It is rich
in maize and yellow pumpkin, but there is no gold
in Apalachen—nor will there be, some say,
unless they count our bones turned gold
in the swamps of this green, accursed land.

Have we more than we were given?

A wheel turns slowly in the beginning;
but as it progresses, the angle grows steeper.

In his third communication to the Emperor Charles V
Hernán Cortés observes that as the breeze was strong
he and his men were able to dash among the native canoes
and break them up and kill and drown many people, and
this to him was the most marvelous sight in the world.

The river which flows across the alluvial plain
does not change its course, but invariably becomes
more characteristic of itself.

Spanish soldiers captured by the Aztecs
were dragged up the steps of the great Cue.
There, at the top, plumes were set upon their heads

and they were given elaborate fans
and were instructed to dance before Huichilobos.
It was only after they had finished dancing
that they were seized and stretched across the altar,
their hearts cut out and their bodies
kicked down the steps to the people, who gathered
expectantly about the pyramid for a taste
of foreign flesh. How does this relate to us?

In discussing the morality of a given action,
it is imperative to remain conscious of tradition.

At Lagos in the 18th century during the vernal equinox
nubile girls were carefully impaled;
and it is said they went to their death willingly,
so persuaded were they by the incantations of the shaman,
convinced they should die that others might live—
a parable to confound the ages.

Our desire to prevent the end of the world
leads irrevocably to human sacrifice.
Now, this first obtains as a primitive gift:
Druidic priests kept criminals and captives
in circular wicker cages designed to represent the sun,
which they set afire to propitiate their god.
But the second means of sacrifice is less overt,
involving, as it does, a living human deity;
from which must follow a frightful implication.

When my brother died I explained to everyone
that he no longer existed. But then it occurred to me
I had been mistaken,
since nothing that once exists may be lost;
nor does anything fail to exist because it has not yet
come into being. I had been betrayed, I could see,

by the limitation of my senses.

Salamanders dwell in regions of fire,
sylphs in the ultimate reaches of space,
gnomes in the earth.
Undines dwell in the sea.

As one drop precipitates
crystal from its fluid,
all dreams resolve.
I am Magus. Trust in me.

It should be emphasized that the route the Pilgrim chooses
to Santiago de Compostela corresponds symbolically
to the central plane of the galactic system—
that irregular span we know must be comprised of stars
and nebulæ invisible separately to the naked eye;
and furthermore is an allegory of the route we follow
to achieve the Magnum Opus.

It is said that Nostradamus experienced a sequence
of visions accompanied by utterances in a tongue unknown
except to him; and he set down all that transpired,
and later, when the ecstasy had diminished
and vatic powers receded, he created acrostic lines;
for if they had stood as simply as he conceived them,
Europe must have staggered and like an earthquake
changed its true perspective. Thus we recognize
how marvels prevent their own completion.

Toward the tribulations of ordinary life
common understanding will suffice,
however ineffectual for philosophic purpose.

The question has been asked whether it is permissible

to evoke the souls of the dead. The immediate response
of the Holy Office is absolute: *Uti exponitur non licere.*
It is forbidden. Still, the hands of the clock do turn,
and it is incumbent upon us to evoke the mighty dead
even as we call upon the resources of the living,
to establish beyond doubt the utter purity of our intent.
Everything else has been but a preparation for this.

Someone just now has inquired concerning
the usage of a device I am building.
I will respond in this way:
When the Greeks were studying the shape of the ellipse
they could imagine no purpose for its shape,
but yet their investigations were requisite preliminaries
to later, eminently practical discoveries.
Therefore, the question is not valid.
When I have completed the fine adjustments
I will show the citizenry where to look;
each then shall be privileged to observe for himself
the phenomenon of which I often have spoken,
which gradually is fading out of sight
and will be lost entirely to our descendants,
diminishing through various causes,
certain of which are explicable, but others less so,
not unlike the magnitude of nations.

We are a tree, as we are its fruit.

The sun rides low in the north, very near to the horizon;
seasons alter. I have a letter from my wife,
who has told our children that I am drowned and
never to come home. Why should I feel as desolate
as I do? All journeys end.

The dolphin can tell if the drowned sailor

ever has tasted dolphin flesh;
if he has, the fish will devour the body ; but if not,
the fish will nudge his body ashore.

Now, whoever is not unacquainted with the writings
and disputes of various philosophers
will acknowledge that no small part of them is spent
on the subject of abstruse ideas. For instance,
according to Cardanus, an emerald placed on the tongue
will assuage the most violent grief.
And yet this is not to be taken literally.

The motion of the head can transmit to the beholder
affection, approval, badinage, curiosity, and remembrance.
The confluence of the hand, head, eye, and brow
results in variations as infinite and filled with meaning
as are the words of a supreme poet.

In certain countries the great masters of any art
will never teach for money.
There are measurements other than those we know.

The mighty river Brahmaputra flows in serene majesty,
and life in the field and village runs smoothly on.

I have been asked upon what form is our earth supported.
I respond that an elephant holds us on his marvelous back.
I have been asked upon what does the elephant place
his feet. I respond that he places them on the shell of
a tortoise. As to the tortoise, what supports him,
I know not.

Indra is Lord of the Heavens.

What should I say next?

We have been told there is a seventh wave which comes in
with higher certainty and magnificence
than its predecessors. But the life that lives
in the depths is not changed; it remains immeasurable,
silent, and oblivious.

Australian scientists reputedly are studying
the carcass of a monster washed up on a remote beach
on the coast of Tasmania. It is almost circular,
and has no eye which can be discovered.
Nor does it possess a head, as such, and it is
empty of bones. The flesh is gelatinous, white,
and rubbery, and is sparsely matted with hair.
The body has been measured: it is twenty feet in length,
eighteen feet broad, and some five feet thick.
Its weight has been estimated at between six
and eight tons. It is like a turtle, but without
appendages, without a shell. I have spoken to a man
who saw this thing, who believes it must be an animal,
although he admits he never has seen a beast
resembling this, nor has heard of anything similar,
and presumes it has survived out of the past.
I believe, to the contrary, it must be a rare monition
of our future state.

Mid-afternoon. Spray sweeps the wooden deck.
Each time we sink within a wave I wonder
if we shall be lifted again, or if we are meant to
descend forever.

Our day lengthens each century
by two thousandths of one second. On its axis
the earth turns ever more slowly; and in years to come
will show always its same face toward the moon.

It happened that when Copernicus of Frauenburg
was about to publish his treatise on the true motion
of the earth, he wrote to a certain Osiander,
who was a Lutheran clergyman of Nuremberg, asking
about the reception such a book might expect.
Osiander replied, saying, first of all it is a fact
that the motion of a planet as it appears to us
may be well enough explained by any of several theories;
and because this is known to the ecclesiastics,
who perceive no harm in such speculation, provided
the originator of a system in conflict with doctrine
does not pretend his hypothesis might be more than
idle fancy, it would be wise of Copernicus
to announce his treatise in some similar light,
by such means to avoid the dangers of controversy:
This the astronomer refused to do. There are few men
of his proportion in any age; there are not many
who will not dissemble. But still, there are these few.

In a Peruvian desert stands the ruin of an observatory
of great antiquity.
Those who employed this place
knew the earth was round,
and began each year
with the rising of the Pleiades.

Gemini stood in the house of Aries
near the equinoctial colure at the moment of Creation.

Within the Sangraal have I witnessed
a man upon whom were the signs of the passion of Christ,
who said: *This is the chalice*
wherein I ate the lamb on Sher-Thursday,
and now thou hast beheld it so openly as thou shalt
in the city of . . .

But this was all I heard; the vision failed.
To this day I do not know if I am meant to rise again,
or if I have come and gone from this holy place
and the time of my redemption is past.

Once again the animals stare with heraldic meaning,
the arrogance of centuries uncurled between their paws.
I am a man from the Middle Ages. My faith is as pure
as a hammer. Especially have I avoided each
sensual pleasure. *Hoc est enim Corpus meum; hic est
Calix sanguinis mei . . .*

Of his jeweled wing the Peacock
is excessively proud, but upon
seeing his black, ugly foot he screams aloud;
so Man, taking pride in vain achievement,
complains and is angered by failure.

The Partridge, being a perfidious bird,
is wont to go away and steal the eggs of another.
But in spite of this she obtains no satisfaction,
because the young, when they are hatched
and hear the cry of their true mother,
run straight to her who has given them birth.
Thus the Devil, who attempts to steal the progeny of God.
When we have heard the noise of our Creator
we understand that we have been stolen
like the children of the Partridge,
and run toward Him who most truly loves us.

Years are reckoned by the passing of winters.

South of Ankara, past the towns of Konya and Karaman
at the edge of an escarpment prior to the Goksu valley,
there is a monastery which dates from the 5th century,

consisting of three buildings: a colonnaded basilica
with a narthex at its entrance, which measures
ten feet in width; a church complete but for the tower;
and a baptistery, all in virtually a perfect state
of preservation. The gate to the basilica displays
what quite well may be the earliest known instance
of the tetramorph: that is, in one single design
a sculpture which unites the symbols of our four
evangelists—the lion of Mark, the angel of Matthew,
the bull of Luke, and the flying eagle of John.
Nearby, on supporting columns, stand the two guardians
of this monastery, the Archangels Michael and Gabriel.
Michael, on the south, tramples underfoot a devotee
of Cybele, the Phrygian goddess, which means
Christianity stands triumphant over paganism.
On the north side, Gabriel is depicted in similar
but more complex design. Forty monks lived here,
ruled by their founder and abbot, whose name was Tarasis.
Of him, little is known, other than that he died
on the 13th of February on the 15th indiction
after the consulship of Flavius Severinus and Flavius
Dagalaiphos, thus dating the settlement at 462.
Scooped out of limestone rock are cells wherein
these monks lived, prayed and studied under the rule
of their abbot. Their lives were, we think, cœnobitic,
which is to say, lived in common. Beautifully preserved
ornaments abound, stone fishes and partridges among them.
But the partridge, as a Christian symbol, has died out
during the centuries which unite and separate these men
from us.

We fully recognize and admit that our completed image
is not merely a reconstruction of separate, constituent,
and unrelated impressions; but rather we tend to perceive
certain shapes and patterns both naturally and readily;

and these we select out of whatever may contain them,
regardless of their disguise.

In days when the discovery of particular marks or signs
was regarded as conclusive proof of a suspect's guilt
the searching for, recognition of, and probing toward
these stigma flowered into an honorable profession.
Shrewd practitioners then, as now, drew a choice
remuneration. Among these was a certain Paterson,
who, having picked his victim totally naked and
rubbed both hands up and down and around the body,
slipped into the quivering flesh a long pin, buried
to the head, and left it there. It was then proposed
to the victim that he locate this pin and draw it out,
which some were able to do, but others were not.
Those who could not find it were seized, numb with
fright, or tearfully protesting their innocence,
and were bound and burnt alive while Paterson stood by
reading aloud the Holy Office. In the town of Elgin
two men were immolated; in Forres, two; at Inverness,
one; and eighteen later on. Paterson was paid
for each, and had two servants, so highly esteemed
were his district prosecutions. Ultimately was learned
what some had always thought, yet never dared to suggest:
that he had not truly represented himself, but was
a pretty woman in male clothing. By innumerable means
we discover our own delight.

The sign may be the figure of a toad or a bat,
the slot of a hare, foot of a frog, a spider,
a malformed whelp, or a mouse. It will be found
under the lip or upon the fundament, if
the suspect be a man. Where women are concerned,
one should meticulously examine the breasts
and pudenda.

Pulvis et umbra sumus.

This noon, I believe it was,
my daughter inquired about our cat, and I
instructed the child to look about.
Together we went outside
and noticed a crowd had gathered
by a huge fire. It seemed
we could hear children screaming,
for which reason we joined the crowd
and there observed a multitude of cats
chained together, ours among them,
being roasted alive. I explained
to my daughter we should have kept our pet
inside, this day on which we honor Saint John.
Are we not dust, and dusty shadows?

A Portuguese on his way from Coimbra
to the University of Paris
fell in with a stranger who offered to teach him
black magic at Toledo, for which lessons
the Portuguese should make over his soul to the Devil
and sign this compact with his blood.
Done, and seven years having passed
the Portuguese continued on his way to Paris
and there obtained quite easily everything he sought.
Later, he burnt his book of spells, scattering the ashes,
and returned to his home, where he took the habit
of Saint Dominic. After a long life
devoted to prayer and to penitence he died at Santarém,
and there his body is venerated to this day.
So also do we render homage
to the weak if they recant, above the strong.

I seem to hear a rattle of chains

and the creak of a galley oars. A voice speaks
in the Oscan tongue:
Does this vessel exist? Or
does it sail across eternity?

Tomorrow at dawn we leave for Sidon and Tyre
and the white harbor, Minet-el-Beida,
that is not far from Ras Shamra, and Ugarit.
Why is the breeze unchanged?
What is the color of gulls in Malabar?

From the East have come Plague, Cholera, and Mankind.
Evil comes from the East, but disappears into the West.

I must look for significance in the past.

It should be noted that in the year 1798
the Bishop of Durham testified before the House of Lords
that the French, having abandoned their plans
for an assault via the channel,
were believed to be plotting a method to undermine
the moral strength of England and so to conquer the Island
by the use of a troupe of costumed dancers!
Yet this will astonish no one who pays attention
to our time.

Thinking brings forth only thought.
Erdachtes kann Gedanken geben . . .

My acquaintance, the Austrian scholar and physician,
is busily writing, although I have been unable to
determine the nature of his subject.
Around us, familiar walls are crumbling, flames spew up
from Europe's chimneys; the night is made hideous
with the shrieks and groans of victims. But

always I hear, if I bend down, the subtle noise
made by his pen scratching across the parchment:
Not only shall we find recession from acute
self-criticism and despair, but that corresponding
loss of imagination, intuition, and sensitivity . . .

It may be that we are entering a state which seems to us
not incompatible with our given ethic,
the true cast of which will prove apparent
in the future, to any child considering us. Perhaps
we already have forgotten how they gestured,
and the sun obscured by ashes, deliquescent currents of
a warm electric wind. To what prayer will you listen,
if not to this?

The creature had no face and only
one limb. Yet it lived
and they had given it their name
because it was born to her.
They had conceived it,
and it existed
by reason of charred events
over which they might have gained
some measure of control;
while the creature,
sighing heavily in its blindness,
seemed also to comprehend.

This day is over.

I could not say where we are, nor indeed
what time it is. I hear someone singing.

The verses of the Kabir have
four different senses:

Illusion,
Intellect,
Spirit,
and the Exotic Doctrine of the Vedas.
Why should a man complain if he is void of understanding?

We know that the word *raga* derives from the Sanskrit
Ramj, which means to color or to dye;
thus the moods of music which color our lives.

It is said of a certain Bengal dancing girl
that she drew rain from the clouds.

It is said that the night *raga*
once was ordered sung at noon.
Darkness descended
and spread as far as the singer's voice.

It seems to me that I am reclining
voluptuously. I have become a woman, yet this
fails to surprise or to alarm me. I am
filled with lassitude, and strange convictions.
Nothing is wrong, but that I am faint and ill
and I am weak with desire.

No man passes my door
toward whom I do not feel the urgency of love.
The stranger who will visit me tomorrow
fills my dream tonight.
From the red tile balcony of my father's mansion
I used often to stare at the harbor.
To my necklace of jewels I will add a charm
for luck.

How should I explain to myself

why everything should so excite me?

I am awake now; it has all been a dream.
Of it I recall only the moon wondrously emerging
from a vestibule between two spreading fronds.
That is enough; from this I divine that soon
I must go down the misty street where blind whores wait,
once more composing my amphigory of lust.

There are certain women who are indolent, greedy,
and carnal, possessed of selfish humors
more treacherous and invisible than channel winds.

I have seen a sarcophagus cast up on the shore
at Fos, and the vessels of Saint Louis
sail out from Aigues-Mortes. How can I explain
why a slender woman excites me?

I know that the toad which lives in prison
is moist to our touch, and flabby
because it does not ever give the steady warmth of love,
but is thus from hidden desire. I no longer deny
cruelties are sweet; there are vines whose tendrils
split cathedral walls.

Warts and fleshly conch,
the butcher's face,
a time is close at hand.
Most of the wicked in cold blood,
next the good in violence;
anger and hours enough
for old regret. Sorrows end.
The toad, emblematic of France,
was born under an early king.

When prophecies are found to be without meaning
those who have sold their possessions
return to untilled fields and looted homes,
broken by the desolation of their hope.
Here, in this anguish for a Second Coming, lies cause
for deep foreboding.

In the year 1198 all Europe was swept with alarm
when it was learned
the Antichrist had been born at Babylon.

A date for the end of the world was fixed by Merlin.
That date was 1970.

Because of the prophecy of Stoeffler, a renowned
mathematician, whose computations enabled him
to foretell the Deluge that should inundate the earth
as high as the mountain peaks, a certain physician
of Toulouse built for himself and his family
an Ark, and provided it with stores of food
and whatever else they should require while waiting
for the waters to subside. What has been done is done.
Yesterday's ignorance and fright become the realities
of our time. Consider the physician of Toulouse.

The moon as it approaches the earth
will raise fantastic tides
that will sweep across the land, engulfing everything
except the highest summits. Yet
Man will not die
because he will have fled and have sent forth
into other spheres the Raven and the Dove.

Noah's Ark is reputed to be

resting on a mountain in Greater Armenia
where the snow falls to such depths
that no man is able to climb through it.
There are those who swear the Ark is visible
at a certain hour, if the day is bright;
or on nights when the moon is nearly full.
They point to an enormous dark object high up
in the snow, where no one ever has been.

Credulity is greatest in times of calamity.

They say that in Mesopotamia
men still dig for the treasure of Nebuchadnezzar,
who grazed like an ox and wet his mortal body
with the dew of Heaven, until his nails turned into claws
and his hair was folded into feathers.

Gradually the future is becoming clear to me;
pathetic difficulties beset those who depart from
traditional assumption.

This is the evening of the 9th day of March.
I have taken pains to record the exact instant
at which the moon obscured a most lovely star
we call Aldebaran. And I note our year: 1497.

According to Pythagoras, we ourselves
are the measure of the universe. If this be so,
pray for us.

The lantern of Augustus has become a storage place
for flowerpots.

I have just found a clay figure, which I believe
represents Saïs. At any cost

I must vary the conditions of my existence!

Two courses diverge before us:
we distinguish them without difficulty. One
we know to be inevitable; and yet
why should we choose either?
Afflictions and evils that befall us
are but adumbrations of tomorrow.

All morning I have spent watching for a sight of land.
It is almost noon.
Birds reel and scream above our ship
and I have heard a voice
which seems to ask if they are more prudent than I,
who never make a sign, but merely wait.

Now there is nothing except the inviolate sea.
The birds have gone, if ever they were here,
and we sail on through endless waters
beneath a gaseous, blue-white austral sun. If only
I knew how it was meant to end, I might begin.

Someone cries out that we have sighted an island
of blue sand. What is the meaning of this?

Hæc omnia tibi dabo, si caudens adoraveris . . .

At first I was incredulous, then puzzled
by the duality of Man. Once it had seemed to me
that whoever revered a high creation must be
generous in his relations with every living thing.
Later, when I had seen more of Mankind,
I did not know what to think. But now I perceive
we are like reeds that grow in water, and
I comprehend this entry in the journal of a soldier:

Yesterday morning we came unexpectedly upon
a group of the enemy who had paused to eat
and laid aside their weapons, which is why
they were unable to defend themselves. We
destroyed them and continued on our way. Winter
is almost over—I look forward to summer
when the rains shall end and flowers appear.

He had been struck in the back as he was
running downhill, and must have leaped forward.
His body lay half-concealed
by the autumn grass, his boots
higher than his head. When we came by
we noticed how his blood had searched the slope,
as though it feared us, and was
endeavoring to find some place to hide.
He was, we think, indifferent to abstractions,
limited in imagination, yet withal,
owning a sharp intellect for minutiæ
of the written law. On the one hand
we doubt he was of sufficient obtusity
that antagonists might outwit him; nor
on the other, pellucid in the comprehension of
his estate. Endowed with ample sincerity
and conviction, he could not ever doubt authority.
And if he had a pleasing manner and a voice
which was modulate, so much the better;
others then could forget the nature of his office.

It is my heart which makes me eloquent; *pectus est*
quod disertos . . .

When we got to the place where the issue was decided
we could distinguish little, except a few yellowish
brick chimneys whose significance we could not guess;

although there had been some evil here, so persuasive
and explicit were these smoking, crumbled ruins—
more articulate than any book, as final as the warriors.

The falconer cannot hold. What is best
seems worst.

Barbarossa sleeps in Thuringia.
In the Kyffhäuser he sleeps at a stone table
attended by six knights
who wait the fullness of time.
Already his beard has grown through the slab;
when it has thrice wrapped around the table
he will lift his head. In that hour
Germany will rise.

Auch das Schöne muss sterben;
even the beautiful must die.

Twelve years have passed.

The keeper explained with an apologetic smile
there was not much to be seen any more,
it had been so long. Brush and weeds had overgrown
the odd cylindrical hut.
I did not tell him I had seen it
once, or that I almost accepted his invitation
to enter, to hang up my clothing on a hook
and refresh myself with a shower
from the painted nozzles.
I did not tell the keeper
I had ever seen this place, since
he failed to recognize me. I am touring
your country, I said, and of course
such things as this are invariably interesting.

It is well known how we are both the creator
and the victim of our universe.
Each sovereign nation conceals within itself a myth
of diabolic force that waits the chosen moment.

God shows a malignant face.

It is said the word *diabolus* derives from *dia*,
meaning two, and *bolus*, meaning pill. The Devil swallows
body and soul.

Certain areas I leave for a purpose.

The mind and body exercise upon one another
reciprocal powers,
the extent of which we do not know.

Lat. 35.28 N.; Long. 17.12 W.
The wind is light.
From the south comes a moderate swell.
I am ill at ease;
I am troubled and full of doubt.
Death has ravished an ancient race.

Now ask my name, who binds men on earth and lays low
fools in the light of day.

Darkly the ravens circle.

Should I yield and bend as Laotze admonishes?
Or resist, as Jacob did?

A physician has told me that in the blood of a man
who devolves into a catatonic stupor
the level of oxygen saturation is remarkably similar

to that of one who has fallen asleep and
is dreaming.

Wir siegen unsere Toten!

The road was lined on either side with stucco barracks,
not one of which had windows. There were willow trees
and beech—yes, and I recall. the administration building
where I was escorted for my interview. I have forgotten
how many men were there, but they were in uniform
with the exception of one—a gray-haired officer
who was dressed in summer clothing. When I
saw him I knew beyond doubt he had been summoned
at the final moment, that he had been ready to depart
for his vacation when someone reminded him of me, and
they had yet to deal with me. This must be the reason
tears gathered in my eyes while I listened to the evidence.
I remember saying to myself I had every right to feel
outraged, not because the charges were untrue but because
these men, who did not know me, none of whom had ever
seen me, should feel their obligation to so arraign me.
It is strange I should not be angered by deceit,
not half so much as that any man could look at me
and say to himself, Thank God!—by tomorrow
I shall be at the shore and can forget about this.

Smoke rises from a chimney; memory oppresses me.

Let the words of Giordano Bruno be struck in stone:
This sentence, delivered in the name of a God of mercy,
is a cause of . . .

The decision, he had been quick to explain,
was not his. Indeed, he whispered, gesturing
with the utmost vehemence and watching us for a sign

of understanding, he thought it unpardonable!—
adding almost at once that if he had possessed
even the slightest degree of authority
he would have countermanded it. Perhaps it is so.
Yet what we recall most often, what was always
most difficult for us to accept, was his anxiety
to impress upon us that he was not to blame.

I would crush these pillars, if I were strong enough,
remembering the hills of Ushita and the woods of Nigitsu.

Wheat has been thrown in the harbor. Whose fault is this?

Voltaire, one morning, following his habitual complaint
that he was about to die, resumed a favorite pastime—
harassing the corpulent priest who waited, perpetually
certain any man ultimately must abjure such heresies—
and muttered while feverishly plucking at the coverlet,
his forehead yellower than a gourd, those small eyes
malignant and evilly coruscate, that howsoever long
we continue to believe absurdities are we doomed to commit
atrocities.

Two centuries ago London was shaken by twin earthquakes
and alarmed by the prophecy of a third
which should totally destroy the city. Now
when the 8th day of March drew near, thousands
fled into the countryside, and those who had scoffed
when they observed the panic were themselves
overcome by terror and could not keep aloof,
but joined the maddened exodus. I will meditate on this.

The ancient Cretans had no word for panic,
nor knew of it in any sense.

Seasons alter, we with them.

What shall I say next? I might mention
that the tomb of Mohammed is miraculously suspended
between Heaven and Earth.

I could announce that whoever owns the Koh-i-Nûr
shall rule the world, provided the owner be a woman.

I could speak of an island called Srirangam
in the river Cauvery, which flows through the state of
Mysore. Close to its western shore
a Hindu temple stands, shut within seven walls,
in whose innermost shrine an idol is seated
whose eyes are the brightest diamonds in the world.
If I went there, Death would not be apt to find me.

 I am like the turtle dove which does not drink clear water
but first muddies the water with its foot,
the better to suit its pensive mind. Have I not seen
what is more valuable than silver, or the hoarded
treasures of Lithuania ? How should I explain ?
Sea-gold and marble columns never have been what I sought,
nor shards of broken amphoræ; but the slightest measure
of myself, and of those who have preceded us across
this desolate shore.

Nothing escapes my notice, except the passage of time.

I set down that the pitch of a violin may shatter a goblet
or bring to the ground a cathedral tower.

I feel it incumbent on me to record how Nicholas Flamel
on the 17th of January, a few minutes before noon,

succeeded in obtaining from one-half pound of purified
mercury a definite quantity of silver, which was adjudged
to be finer than any the king got out of the royal mine.

I will set down that the history of the Orloff
has been lost in the mysterious imaginations of men,
and the date of its entry into our affairs is not known.
Some assert it is the Great Mogul, seen only once
by Western eyes; yet there are others who believe
these two are separate gems and the Mogul will reappear
undiminished in the palm of a native child.

I shall here record the existence of an island called
Java, where nutmeg grows, together with spikenard,
pepper, galingale, cloves, cubebs, and precious spice,
and women are kind, where sorrows end.

Last night a woman took me to her bed.
I explained to her that in the desert there is a place
called Oudan, and I must go to Oudan. She replied
that by morning I would have forgotten.

It seems to me now I am in some Slavic land
where it is summer. Clouds fly overhead
 as I have not seen them since I was a child.
Near the hilltop a young girl
is standing, and beside her a boy
whose long hair is blowing in the breeze.
She begins to sing, and dances for his pleasure.
Trees are dark against the sky,
pale yellow flowers adorn the hill.
I think of pigeons in a courtyard
fluttering and clapping their wings,
By the castle road in winter,
by the castle road in spring . . .

Suddenly I am in a Roman attic; a young man
I met on the banks of the Tiber has invited me.
I was reluctant, though I could not say why;
it was plain he loved me. Now he has
quickly, furtively, put on an elegant
brocaded robe, and shows me the wonder
of his pale gynandrous thigh, motioning me
to come to him where he indolently reclines.
It seems that we are flying. And is there
some reason I should feel alarmed?

I have just this instant waked up.
The ship is rolling across heavy seas.
From the porthole I discern nothing but interminable fog
and spray that flings itself against the gelid glass.
There are no voices, nothing
save the creak of timber. God knows
where we are bound.

When Columbus landed among the Antilles
he could not have been aware that to the north of him
like a tapestry the last Viking colony of the New World
was fading coldly out of sight. I must meditate
further on this.

It was the figurehead which gave soul to Norse
longboats—carved of soft wood
in the form of prodigious serpents whose burning gaze
streamed outward from the bow. Truly
we are lost. *Pater noster, qui es in cœlis . . .*

Mankind yearns for annihilation.
The earth shall revert to worms and the rolling sea
to plankton.

Lat. 28.40 N.; Long. 60.10 W.
I reflect on the second Bishop of Yucatán, by whose zeal
we have lost all knowledge of the Mayan glyphs.
Of thousands of illuminated manuscripts on sized-agave
paper, only three were saved from this vandal cleric.

It is said that Almagro climbed the Andes, losing
one hundred and fifty Spaniards and ten thousand Indians
to the snow. Six months later, upon his return,
he found them standing where they had been left,
singly, and in groups, tightly holding the bridles
of their ice-bound horses. Tell me, who has computed
their share of Paradise?

Come closer.
Listen. I transcribe
reality for you.

We know that somewhere on the plateau of Bogotá
exists a band of savages which annoints its chief
with oil, and showers him with gold dust
until he is gilded and is known as El Dorado.
Let us march forth to discover him
where he stands, alone and regal in the August noon.

Against the center of the furthermost wall of a temple
containing a single chamber in the ruined city of
Chichen, long lost beneath the jungles of Yucatán,
is the figure of a man with a symmetrical beard and
powerful Hebraic features. Various theories account for
his presence, yet thinking brings forth only thought.

A toucan is reported, more than a century old,
which lives in the jungle and had belonged to Indians
and learnt their language. Now this tribe is extinct,

so that of all things on earth there is only this bird
which can speak the words these people spoke, and has
no idea of their meaning.

In northern Panama there are Indians which are called
Guaymis, whose chiefs wear a resplendent headdress
of feathers obtained from the Quetzal, sacred bird
of the Aztecs. These men are small, with reddish skin
and flat faces, and they assault invaders with
a throwing stick, the *m' adtli*. They wear necklaces
made of jaguar and peccary teeth and human scalps.
It is said that one, after he had been captured
by Spaniards, and tortured, and was ready to die,
gazed up at the cross which they held above him,
and inquired in his native tongue if he would find
Christians in Heaven, for which deliberate blasphemy
they scorched his bones. Thus, we also live again
the conflicts of our inheritance.

Discipline, threats and blows are required; by the usage
of such methods the mind of any man
can be induced to surrender itself of arrogance.

When Bartolomé de las Casas had demonstrated
to his countrymen how they had been guilty
of outrageous crimes against humanity
he was himself attacked, and the historian
Saavedra y Fajardo, as well as numerous captains,
priests, and counselors testified
to the plentiful harvest of souls,
saying conquest is ethical
and injustice cannot exist which follows
close upon the order of authority.
Nor is anything more holy than a war
which is fought in the purity of high intent.

This argument is entered.
Lá vão os pés onde quer o coração.

We are told the ocean is no more than forty leagues,
but still we know these people are mendacious
and would give everything they possess
to witness our end. God knows why. Is this our thanks
for having staked our lives in South Sea hurricanes,
hacked a trail through pestilential jungle
and miasmic swamp to bring the message of Our Redeemer?
Some say we would have been wiser to stay at home
and let these filthy savages roast in Hell.
Such is gratitude. From our plateau
the escarpment breaks away in violet, umber, and saffron
struck with hues of richest red. Clay and
sandstone turrets, totems, effigies,
and narrow granitic mountains loom further
than any of us can see. The land is bountiful,
but yet there is a sense of doom. Malignance plays
about our souls. We have marched three full months;
we suffer from the east wind and the cold.
Our fires are small. They look pitiful in this place
where snow falls incessantly. Vallejo has sworn
October snow falls less quietly in Castile.

Pray for us.
Ora pro nobis.

Even now I do not know what was said
to convince me, unless
it may have been whispers of another country
beyond Quivira, which they call Arae,
and beyond this another whose names is Guaes,
which also is marvelous. We believe
Arae must be a most rich' prize; but as for

this place called Guaes, my friend,
Moctezuma's treasure is fit for dogs.

In a moment we shall cross the equator.

He had been mortally struck,
and as I stood gazing down on him
he wept, and said he would die.
The wound was not bleeding
half so profusely as others I had seen;
still, it seemed to me
I should not argue with him.
So it was I asked why he had volunteered
to come on such a voyage as this.
He answered it had been necessary
and thereupon he stared hard at me and I
discovered that he was dead.
Asking again my same question,
why he had lifted up his name for this;
he answered me again, and said
he had done so out of admiration for his leader
saying he knew nothing of the world
and was overcome with admiration
for the fine eloquence and authority of the leader.

We utter words and
hear them
and they pass by. And we say
this is a lengthy stanza.

We long have recognized as an indisputable fact
that during the Middle Ages the Moors drove westward
seven Portuguese bishops who crossed the Ocean Sea
and founded the Seven Cities of Antilia. For this reason
Cristóbal Colón, Admiral of the Ocean, gave this name

to certain islands of the Caribbean; and therefore
we are not wrong if we assume it is but a matter of time
before we part the leaves of one tree, or sail beyond
a final point to discover these citadels before us,
and be blessed.

Pedro de Alvarado founded the Spanish city of Guatemala
the same year Hans Holbein painted the *Dance of Death*.

All rivers flow east. Leaves
rest on the mountain.

I pause, listening to the state of my excitement,
and discover it to be not only prodigious
but increasing! I await some further intimation
that shall burgeon richly inward.

I have heard it said that one man, living alone,
by the intensity of his conviction may ignite the earth.

My brother just now has paused in his work to ask
what I am doing, and the reason. He believes
my life would be less unacceptable if I should labor
toward some profit, or loss, as fortune wills.
I have explained to him, but he is puzzled.
I am gathering, in order to collate, what otherwise
must be scattered and left anonymous by the maelstrom,
tenderly, with a sense of profound obligation.
I have rescued from oblivion many things
that have no name, and there are more. My brother
stands silently, not far away, regarding me.
In a moment he will ask to whom I may be obligated.

As the earth turns,
each life turns.

Where are they painted
that were drowned,
who had taken their vows?

South of the Florida Keys on a Cuban beach
five shipwrecked priests are known to have buried
the fabulous jeweled robes of the Virgin of Yucatán.
Missum quod nescitur non amittur; losses that are
unknown are no loss at all.

Because I have despaired of love, and Christianity
is a box of futile toys, I have studied
Finnish magic and the sorceries of Lapland,
have informed myself concerning the Bersekir of Iceland,
the Shaman of Siberia, the Mutang of Korea, and
Serbian lycanthropy.

Roumanian farmers put up each night
a few brambles on the lintel, and new turf
on the sills. In this way
it becomes impossible for a demon or hag to purchase
entry.

John Baptist Cibo, who was elected to the papacy
under the designation of Innocent VIII,
being sincerely alarmed by the prevalence of witchcraft,
issued the bull of 1488
calling upon the nations of Europe
to rescue the Church of Christ from the powers of evil,
detailing sorcerous afflictions, blighted marriage-beds
and the blasting of corn and the fruit of the trees
and herbs of the field,
appointing inquisitors in every country
armed with apostolic powers;
and thereby did more to augment

the reach and vision of everything he abhorred
than any man who ever lived.
This, also, has its parallel in our time.

Saint Philip Neri was able to distinguish heretics
by their odor. Upon being met with one
in a public street he was obliged to turn away his head
from the noxious emanation.

No one is bound to accuse, or to incriminate, unless
it is before God. *Accusare nemo se debit, nisi cora, Deo.*

The transmutation of base metal into gold,
symbolic of our quest, is said to be accomplished
by means of a miraculous plant
which grows on the slopes of Mount Lebanon.
In the month of May, after the last snow has melted
this plant appears, invisible by daylight
but glowing like a torch in darkness.
The leaves disappear when we attempt to remove them.
In this way, the allegory is complete.

Let us doubt without unbelief of things to be believed.
These are the words of Saint Augustine.

It seems to me that I am calling—gesturing
and hurrying toward a man I never have seen;
but when I reach him he is altered,
turned into a monument! I cannot think what to do,
and look around and see another man
slumbering at my feet; but as I stoop to waken him
I discover that he is made of stone!
I am lost in some antediluvian forest. Tangled branches
of long-fallen trees prevent me from escaping.
I have guessed what this means: each of us

is bitterly and perpetually deceived.

Credulity is greatest in times of calamity.

It was the 24th day of August
shortly before noon, as nearly as we can tell.
In the vaults where they had gathered,
cast into one ineffable mold,
eight families were unearthed,
more rigid than marble—
variegated and temperate now—keeping close watch
over their petrified food, jewels, and candelabra.

Mirabile visu!
Is it not marvelous
both to see
and to relate?

I have agreed to paint a narrative on the city walls.
I have now been at work many years,
there is so much to be told. I have painted,
among other things, an evening in December
with a sky that is smokily overcast
and dry winds rippling through barren trees.
I have painted my sister—bloodied, shaven and
dressing in moldering rags—as she was led
out of her cell. I have painted her among the others.
The Angel of Death is there—in culotte skirt
and riding boots, carrying a leather whip
in a white-gloved hand. I have painted my sister
singing to the Angel of Death, who listens
with evident pleasure. When the song has ended
my sister must walk through a door to the furnace
where fiery clouds belch from a luteous chimney.
God the Avenger sees everything.

The world is deep and deeper
than daylight may reveal.
Die Welt ist tief und tiefer
als der Tag gedacht.

Henrik Holck on the way to claim his bride
dreamt he was offered a sword in place of her.

My grandfather spoke of having seen him twice,
once walking in the courtyard
and once in the royal antechamber
upbraiding the King. Now, the statues in his image
have been broken and their pieces hauled away.
The house in which he lived is gone,
and the cemetery where his wife was buried.
Gone is the site of his own burial.
A few legal documents remain, his testament,
and one madrigal we sing.

They say that I gazed down at him with indifference;
but I remember only that he lay on his back,
one leg slightly bent, with one hand resting
on the pommel of his sword—the other outstretched
as though he had been reaching for a blade of grass.
His mouth filled up with blood as I stood over him;
it ran across his lip and hurried down his cheek,
staining the white collar and the eagle.
They tell me I kicked the body and spat
and made an obscene gesture, and hurried on my way.
I have been considering, since then, what I should do
with my life—because I cannot go on like this.

Pause.
Begin again.

The ship lies at anchor.
It is three in the morning.
Palms no longer creak in the wind.

A spider dangles above me in the darkness
of this austral night.

Gross hallucinations trouble me. Seasons end
that I shall not have but once.
My soul is filled with
light, slow currents among sporaceous shadows of
an earlier need.

Yesterday at low tide
I came upon a long bronze casket
almost buried in the sand, richly salt-encrusted.
I meant to open it, but a gull appeared
wheeling and screaming
each time I fondled the ancient lock.

A race is not quick to lose its memory
of the past
through dark centuries
or upon foreign ground. Traditions grow obscure and
more obscure at every year.
Alien strains engraft themselves
on old legends
in puzzling and strange fashion.

Visible changes come slowly
or not,
as we wish.

Soon it will be four in the morning.

If I resemble some other man, who can describe
how inwardly I am possessed by narcotic visions? We
are born and we die. Not one of us recalls
the significance of his birth;
equally do we stay unaware of the intimations
of our death. How should we accept the Seasons of God?

It is said that by the quiet use of
our hands,
even those among us who are most baffled and tormented
may find some measure of peace.

Strolling singers who roam the earth telling of
their need, returning thanks,
find always, south or north, someone
skillful at song, open-handed and generous,
until all things vanish; light and life
passing together.

Have I hunted with Swedes and Hrethgoths
or sung songs with Eomanric,
who gave me this ring?

I know that I may employ flowers of sulphur for the lungs,
sarza for the liver, and castoreum for
those intricate passages which associate the brain;
nor have I yet denied the efficacy of these.
Still, my questions go unanswered. But there is one I
do not hesitate to ask again.

Have you seen him? Has he come this way?

If, by chance, you meet,
say that a Christian
whose name you have forgotten

was inquiring,
but could not wait.

They had laid him between two rows of candles
bending down
from a south wind that entered
through primitive, medieval fenestration. Magic of gold
and flowers!—a recollection of Cistercian monks
comforted me as I looked on him
this final time, whom I have loved.
I thought he was not asleep, but only simulating;
that scarred and pitted face retained
the look I knew so well,
of pensive, unperturbed meditation. The king never dies.

Rex numquam moritur.

Thou art Peter,
and on this rock will I build my church.

It is incumbent on me to establish some image whereby
all men must judge
future interpretations, believing
in the value of mine. This I do tenderly, humbly,
and with the knowledge of utter obligation.

Whitsunday.
The sky is bleak. Birds overhead.

I cannot be sure if I am awake, or sleeping.

The fishermen are dead; we do not know the cause.
It seems to us their boat is scorched,
as though they had sailed far to the south
where the vertical rays of the sun prove fatal.

The community of victims is necessarily identical
to that which unites them with their executioner.
Da amantem et sentit quod dico; a similar lover will
understand.

We know how the intellect comes into play only upon
the command of lower faculties, which are
thought, memory, and imagination.
When these have been aroused, the intellect is stirred.

Lalle, Bachera, Magotte, Baphia,
Dajam, Vagoth , Heneche Ammi Nagaz . . .

In cases of extreme dæmonic possession
the features of the victim become contorted with hate;
he, or she, experiences headache and vertigo;
instinct and functions are flung into disorder;
there is a tendency to prophesy; witnesses describe
a chill wind that emanates from surrounding walls.
I have set this down promptly, in saffron letters,
because of its importance.

A wax model of a woman rests in a glass case
on a bed of cinders. The wax is smeared,
the hair has been torn out, the limbs are broken
and the features melted together. That which we destroy
abides within us.

Neither soldiers nor peasants become the founders
of a noble race; natural laws have been defined.

The Governor having arrogated to himself a conscience
that seeks to displace my own, I have no choice
but to refuse. Were I to acquiesce
I should be no wiser than fragments of amphoræ

scraped from the harbors of Tunisia.

I have seen an object clinging to a cliff
with nothing about it for miles in any direction
except the sky, the sea, and primeval rock.
Even the fish have divined its presence and lean
motionless beneath their natural depths.
Only men are there, to burnish and praise it.

Who is your authority? Who
is he?
Who has granted you the right to leave us like starfish
shriveling on a blistered beach?

He explained to us how he chanced to be in this
situation, and the reason he was obligated
to deal with existing conditions, assuring us
most eagerly that under favorable circumstances . . .

Our lives we pledge! Our fortunes! Our sacred honor!

Kraepelin has described paranoia as the endogenous
insidious development of a
permanent, unshakable, delusional system
with complete preservation of clarity in thought,
will, and action.

We spoke with them at great length, but came away
knowing only that they believed their course
to be clear, their duties plain. Their vision
was not obstructed, as is our own, by niggling doubts
or pernicious hesitation.

It is mid-afternoon, yet there is almost no light
beneath the trees clogged by vines, growing with

such fantastic rapidity it seems they have altered
while we stood here whispering. We advance with caution,
it is so dark and filled with adumbrations of tomorrow.
There is a deserted hut, thatched with palm, veiled
by slack spider webs. We move among ashes white as pewter,
broken bowls, pools of mephitic water; and sense
forgotten evils here. Among the treetops something
moves restlessly. Beyond the vacant hut, ringed
by unpainted sticks, we observe what must have been
a grave. The light we shoot aloft proves what we
have suspected, and delicately clattering instruments
which monitor the exploration ceaselessly apprise us
it should not be long. Memories oppress us.

This was the site of our capital; there was none
more beautiful in the civilized world.

We have seen the pastel tunics of countless men;
the fabric is lustrous—indeed,
marvelous to behold! Yet some say they are but figures
swiftly drawn for a new Goyesque caprice!

Who has shifted onto me this prodigious weight?

My brother in the wisdom of his conceit
is not willing to admit that my ingenuity
is mathematically, inevitably, equivalent to his own;
since we are not separate entities, but one.
And therefore our two accomplishments are one.
He believes I cannot solve the acrostic of his fortress;
but yet it is self-evident that I must,
because we both have drawn the plan.
He believes the perimeter of my argument has
wrinkled like the wattle of a beaten cock,

not realizing this must be his also. I am he,
wrapped in identical conceit: what he does
have I done; what I do, has he accomplished.
Thus, we near the end of our cloistral journey.

Terror exceeds contrition; meticulous horror sings
its high Euclidean song.

Archæologists have discovered a lens
of pre-Christian origin;
we know that through a primitive telescope
Cæsar viewed the coast of Britain.

This day has ended.

Since dawn I have been reading on the subject of
miraculous healings, apparitions,
and similar phenomena. Now, one Catherine Labouré
was visited on numerous occasions by the Madonna,
who said in response to her complaint that a certain
Father Aladel chose not to believe in Labouré's account
of these same manifestations:
Be calm, my child. The day will come
when he will do what you ask for.
He is my servant and would not dare to displease me.
With this, the visitation ended.
It is significant that whereas mystics speak
in unknown tongues and variously confound
each hostile witness, particular truths endure.
And of these, one is the unicity of the individual.
Because Labouré had been a servant, we question
whether it was the Madonna or a menial that spoke.
Even so, it is imperative to accept the principle
of miraculous intercession, since by ourselves

we could not help but superintend our dispossession.

Apparitions are a reminder; they constitute a warning.

According to the biography of Saint Teresa of Avila,
an angel pierced her heart with a spear that burned
with a point of fire. It is known that after her death
the heart was examined by twelve reputable physicians,
who discovered on its surface a mysterious white fissure.

Hinton considers us potentially of further dimensions.
Here, again, I demonstrate the imprint of my necessity.

The practice of exsanguination was greatly augmented
by the celebrated announcement of William Harvey,
which cannot surprise whosoever has chosen to contemplate
the Alphabet of Man.

Pliny informs us that the Garden of the Hesperides
will be found on the Atlantic coast of Africa
in the estuary of Loukkos, on the site of Lixus.
But I have been there; and I found only a box
floating with the tide, bright with promise,
precious to all Mankind—which is the reason
I hurried forward. But I was too late, and beheld it
drift away, knowing it never had been meant for me
but another man—emptied of dreams and loss,
orisons, symbols, and a vision of the equinox
who will set forth, not as I would sail from Greece
to Colchis.

How does it come about that each of us devises
some differing manner in his own mind to worship
what he loves?

We consider among the shadows
of mid-morning
what had been announced in terms of light.
I recall the heads of Entremont
and Roquepertuse! *Exorcizio te, immundissime spiritus,*
omne phantasma . . .

It has been recorded that the outbreak of the Korean war
precipitated numerous suicides in the city of Hiroshima.

Ominous revelations, delivered by a multitude
of hallucinatory voices
impinge upon these meditations: Sodom and Gomorrha
have been destroyed by subterranean
explosions of compressed gases and deposits
of petroleum.

What should I say next?

Inside a hollowed oak I once found the remnants
of a leather bag containing five bronze coins
bearing the emblem of a bull with lowered horns,
many silver pieces from the time of Vespasian,
a solid gold amulet of marvelous design, and jeweled
medals carrying the inscriptions of Gordian, Julia Pia,
and Gallienus. Now it seems strange to me that this
was not enough.

Waxen, yellowed masks are doctored by living hands
to simulate the grimace of life, when there is none.

Songs of love are sung
appropriate to the holocaust.

Shall I set my wages on the Wheel of Fortune, or not?

Nothing is better calculated to invite us
to live as we ought, according to the friar
Roger Bacon, who are born and raised
in this life of grace, than to see men deprived of grace
reach incalculable dignity
through the holiness of their lives.

I have heard of a certain man that never spoke
for twenty years, who could not be influenced by an age
that failed to participate in him. Perhaps
the mockery of the populace sounded less consequent
to his ear than the passage of each April breeze.

The greatest of pleasures, I have heard, is
privilege. This may be,
I do not know. It has a plausible sound.

Yesterday I attended the theater. I seated myself,
thinking I must be early. Perhaps I fell asleep, I
do not know; I assert only that when I lifted my head
the columns had fallen, weeds withered among
dusty marble tiers, and glaucous lizards rhythmically
were breathing the somnolent noon; and it seemed
I was in Tunis. What meanings might obtain from this?
There could be several.

My friend, the Historian, has explained
how his most fertile pods quite often are those
wherein coexist seeds out of curiously varied fields;
and yet, contrarily, he added, I do not mean
we bring necessarily into close conjunction
processes that obviously are disparate. Not, that is,
for this condition but none other.

I have spent the night drawing premonitory figures.

I have drawn the picture of a dog
but like a lion rampant—that is, standing
on its sinister hind leg with forelegs elevated,
the dexter above, its head in profile,
with a mane and frightful teeth and every feature
of a lion. Now it is morning; I see
what I have drawn and it is a lion. Yet
a dog appeared to me, which I drew; and all night
while I labored, Death stared across my shoulder
waiting for me to hesitate. Visions are seldom
without some usage.

A boy appeared, not more than twelve years of age,
with a fair complexion, plump and continually smiling,
with that strangely sweet odor of youth, and
affable resignation to the demands of his elders
one perceives, now and then, in boys of moderate
disposition. He entered obediently
as soon as he was summoned, and stood before us
deferentially, gazing not at us but at the floor.
He seemed a little more shy, perhaps,
than other boys his age—on account of that singular
quality, we think, that brought him to our attention.
He was asked to look at each of us,
so we might see for ourselves what we had been told.
After some slight hesitation,
as though he fully knew what this might mean,
the boy did lift his head and, in utter silence,
looked our direction. Although we had been warned
what to expect, we were horrified. It was true,
the eyes of the child were gazing inward.

It is to be understood that there exists
a mystic correspondence between the organs of the body
and the several parts of the Universe.

The head is in accord with the Ram, the feet with
Fishes, and so through the signs of the Zodiac.

I am held in thrall by a thousand things! Last night
while studying a cluster of lights I imagined
a constellation which extended from Achernar to Megrez;
so that no matter where I stood, some reaches
must remain beyond me.

The diameter of Antares is reputed to be
four hundred and twenty million miles. Hours pass by;
each is reckoned against us.

Pereunt et imputanter.

Though it is known to visit every man
tragedy shall be recreated only by one
born of the mass and weight of human suffering,
who cannot but purify himself
in the unending struggle against his destiny.

When there is no creed opposed to argument
there can be no heresy, and persecutions flower feebly.

Certain faces grow familiar down the course of history.
Imprisoned because they could not agree to prevailing
opinions were, among others, Rousseau and Diderot,
Voltaire, Defoe, Pepys, Knox, Wycliffe, Cervantes,
Calderón—is there some reason to continue? What is this
but a ceaseless narrative?—told by kings and peasants.

Who is that in the golden helmet
who rides over wind and water? Tell me, if you know,
and I will announce the date that winter sets
in Babylon.

Near the close of the 16th century
a date was fixed for the end of the world,
when all men should be turned to karyaster
and the earth itself to vapor. That date has come
and gone; yet it was the same year and
near to the very day when, for the first time
in recorded history, an entire city suddenly
disappeared as though struck by the breath of God.
Thus, beginnings notify their end.

It is said that the loss of one life is easily grasped,
or the loss of ten, or of one hundred,
but that the loss of all the inhabitants of the earth
is much too vast for comprehension; but still
the assimilation of this is not requisite,
for on the instant such a catastrophe occurs
none would be left to marvel or lament. It is my belief
this is no less irrelevant than to argue over the noise
a tree makes falling in the forest where no man is.
I am not able to accept the loss of one life,
nor is there any gaoler I do not abhor,
beside whose name I fail to inscribe perpetual guilt,
nor on whose grave I would place so much as a stick.

Should I imagine a faith without reason?

We are told that forty stallions,
together with forty virgins in jeweled garments,
were slain on the grave of Genghis Khan!

Goats and camels sing
and cymbals ring!
Rarely do thoughts of love disquiet me.

Women have drunk their incessant dream of love from me

and would eat my heart, if I offered it.

My brother cannot admire any man
who professes to adore a woman: when he hears it said
a sly smile comes across his face. I know him
to be a libidinous, sensual man, extremely tender-hearted,
who cannot bear to injure anyone. Are such complexities
more needless than they seem?

We are told of the female eel, which is
so overcome with lust
that she is willing to become pregnant by a serpent,
and for this reason can be summoned with a hiss.

The Church, in its struggle with the lusts
of Man, takes care to achieve no ultimate victory,
since then there could be
but little justification for its perpetuity.

It is incumbent on me to record
the agony of Saint Simeon, who pressed an iron belt
into his ulcerous flesh.
I must speak also of Macarius, naked
in the mephitic swamp. But above all others
I mention the agony of Jerome
who slept unremittingly the powerful dream of women.

I have just now waked up!
There is a presence outside my door;
I hear someone breathing.
Lalle, Bachera, Magotte, Baphia . . .

The night is brilliant.
With the advent of darkness I become
more masculine and confident.

Women are not unaware of this. They are aroused
when they least anticipate, and give forth
a singular fragrance,
neither too subtle nor imperious.
The night is beautiful,
and pleasures lie in secret.

Warm winds blow across my body, and odors
from the tropic shore. I hear the sound of a woman's voice
which has carried over the water.
I am sick of contemplation. I feel the need of
pleasure.

All that remain of her visit are these: a few
petals, an opened brooch,
a glove,
and a ruby on the floor
near the veil
I, with such violence, had torn away.

According to the Upanishads, they that see variety
and never unity
shall suffer many deaths.

Lajjita, which is modesty,
is a downward glance, the lashes meeting.
Saci, that which is
secret, we convey by glancing steadily from the narrowest
corner of the eye. *Vira*, the heroic,
is a radiant glance. It is open, direct, majestic
and controlled,
with the iris immobile.

The wind has died away. There is not a sound.
I will sleep now; I am at rest.

The sea this morning is gray-blue in color
like some half-forgotten gown.
I cannot say what this portends.
The birds have flown; we watched them yesterday
bending eastward
carefully, silent and intent,
full of knowledge too subtle for human apprehension.

Hours divide.

Noon. I have gathered murex and green abalone.

It is summer overhead and along the shore.
There is not a sound except the lapping of water
as if even the tide were undecided.
I might linger where I am. Idly
I wonder, and wait.
Have I been here so long,
suspended like an insect in this austral breeze,
dreaming the lengths of meridians,
that I could not, even if I wished, reach the coast of
Timor Laut? There is time enough. Tomorrow
will be soon enough.

I have been happier these past few days
than I have ever been.

This morning, at the furthest point of the reef,
we discovered the wreckage of a foreign ship.
The masts had splintered and fallen.
Bolts of embroidered cloth surged in the water
and a casket of mahogany tilted emptily toward the sky.
The port from which this vessel sailed
we do not know. The hull
was unadorned; not a word was written anywhere.

Die Kunst ist lang und kurz ist unser Leben.

In the sand we have come upon two fragments of rotted wood
on which there are traces of what may once have been
white paint, turned aureate by the sun. My brother thinks
these were sticks lashed together to fashion a cross;
but I have told him they signify nothing, and our day
is quickly over.

My beginnings seem to me far away.
Countless things have intervened; I have loved
so little, and yet so much, that I can barely speak.
I have taken accurate note of each, although
each of its self was meaningless,
aware that within me each would exist for a purpose
past comprehension. I took note and waited,
patiently, for that shock which creates
the transillumination of temporal matter,
as crystal is of an instant formed in treated water.
Thus I have waited. Life goes on, and days
draw swiftly in.

At the bottom of each layer of certain shales
in Oeningen are blossoms of poplar and camphor,
harbingers of the vernal equinox. Above these
are tiny, winged summer ants, and leaves of elm.
Wild grape, plum, and the camphor's autumn fruit
complete this varve. Thus each year is fixed
and printed, as it were, by the lithography of Nature.

I would speak of the seasons, but there are none in me.

Years of abstinence, rectitude, and growth.
We are a tree
as we are the fruit.

Vorbei sind diese Träume.
This day has ended.

Methods of argument leading
out of one expression toward another
may not be worn from the passage of centuries;
I will explore new and uncertain ways,
starting from sensuous perception.

Lat. 30.16 S.; Long. 120.10 W.
The water here is like rose quartz
or bloodstone
as though we had anchored on a bed of coral.
Even our ship takes on a radiant hue.
This world is bright
and things we fail to dream . . .

A broad leather belt swiftly was strapped across his face;
at this he stiffened, but otherwise could not move.
The mask extended from the center of his forehead
to his chin; in it were two slits, one for the nostrils,
the other for his lips.

I communicate directly. I would speak discreetly if
there were time.

Dhia Bith leat chun an ath Chlach Mhile
agus na's fada. God be with you to the last milestone
and beyond.

It is well known how didactic poets, investing each
judgment with beauty, appeal to the young.

It has been noted that dramatists, poets, and composers

are like spiders which produce great works
by the meticulous spinning forth of their entrails.

Juan de Echelar created a candle
from the arm of an infant strangled before baptism
and lighted the tips of the fingers,
which are said to have burned with a perfect flame.
What is the meaning of this?

Darkly the river wells from a sudden orifice;
I am not strong enough to channel the turbid waters
which subside, only to pour forth again
while I least anticipate.

When the infamous Marquise de Brinvilliers had been burnt
and of her body nothing remained except noxious smoke,
odors, and residue, the populace collected handsful
of her ashes to treasure; and Sévigné observed
that now she had become part of the atmosphere, meaning
all of us breathe malevolence from the past.

When the saints have reigned an even thousand years
the earth, regenerated by fire, again shall be habitable.

Are there measurements of time other than those we know?
Some speak of a Capuchin in the forest
who paused an instant to listen to one bird sing,
and returning to the convent gate
found none remembered him, he had been gone so long.

In Persia there is a city called Saveh
from which the Magi went forth to worship Christ.
The Magi are buried in Saveh
in three sepulchers. It is reported their bodies

are yet whole, and their beards still grow.

A man with a red beard is not fit to be a doctor.
A spider hung around the neck is protection from ague.

When I was young I did not know whether to become
a musician, an artist, or a professor of medicine.
To have no belief is to suffer.

From the University of Montpellier
where the disciples of Avicenna were rude to me
and belittled me, I traveled to Seville.
But I was not at home there, no matter what they say.
Oh, yes, I have visited Salamanca
and have seen the Sorbonne
and everywhere met with fools!
I believe there must be one wise man,
and I will travel until we meet,
or Death rides from the gate of Helsingfors.

What have we done with our lives but earn money, connive,
and slander, as we await the dawn?

Some say Judas acted not for silver,
but to hasten that moment when he would be redeemed.

Stewed bats, goat blood, ground horn of animals,
webs, viper lungs and roots,
bark and powdered jewels
we faithfully administered,
meanwhile praying for his Soul.
But on the fourteenth day, in great agony,
he was observed to surrender up the Ghost.
How could we have done more?

Tonight on the church road the moon
looks colder than I ever have seen it,
and mist obscures the valley.
It is a long way to Jutland
in this year of Our Lord
1602. Save me from Evil, I
who am the Prince of Medicine
and Philosophy, chosen of God
to extinguish and blot out delusion.
My fame has spread throughout
this world. Crowds everywhere
gather about me. Virgins offer
their bodies, and old men
their works. Who can say why
children are not impressed?

Each thought I set down
and stamp with its appropriate color,
that there be no mistake.
Of mistakes there can be none;
we lack the time for emendation.

It is not long past that I entered a country
renowned for the quality of its horses.
But everyone to whom I there addressed myself
 said these animals were of meager account,
and there were horses descended from Bucephalus,
which are born like him, with a horn
on the forehead; and I would distinguish
the print of their hooves in the morning sod
if I would but travel another league.
For advice, I courteously thank every man.
I seldom have need to remark on my plans.
Why should I tell strangers I expect to travel

until I have come at last to that holy city
which is called Byzantium? Now, if you are able,
speak my name.

Of precepts and didactic teaching,
little remains.

What shall I trade for a basket of Brazilian diamonds?

What is the price of a pearl
from Coromandel?

What is more precious than Xanadu,
or a galleon
steeply balanced with Indian gold?

Have I been asleep? If so,
the substance of what I dreamt
I cannot tell,
nor of tomorrow; or if either might bring us
a moment closer to Redemption.

That which was our beginning
we have named the Creator,
and our whole history is a rhythm
and a cycle which is made
out of our procession and our return.

Four suns have appeared in the African sky;
a woman has given birth to the head of a black calf.

In the year 1162 the maiden Alan-goa,
ravished by a moonbeam, gave birth to Genghis Khan.

There is nothing I hesitate to summon out of the past

if it may suffice to prevent or mitigate our future.

On the 28th day of November in the year 2349
before Christ, a comet cleaved the plane
of the earth's orbit beneath the meridian of Pekin,
where Noah dwelt. The mountains of Armenia were shaken
to their foundations, wellsprings of the deep
were opened, and rain dropped and continued until
it reached a depth of six and one-quarter miles.
Let us doubt without unbelief of things to be believed.

In the Middle Ages it was held that songbirds
migrated during particular seasons of the year.
But in the 18th century this was totally disproved
and the medieval mind exposed to steep ridicule.

There is no faith more impenetrable than skepticism;
nations fail with the complicity of citizens.

It is said that during the metamorphosis of England
from pagan traditions to the Christian faith
there came a refinement of values, ordering the currents
of life, coloring the devices of imagination.
From primitive epics to Apocryphal themes,
martyrologies, dream-visions, prophetic verse,
and hymns of adoration, the mood was altered;
wherefrom we are taught of the shaping energy and
strength of Christian learning, of the power
of Biblical exegesis and the omnipotent liturgy,
of Hexæmeral tradition, of dogma and of doctrine.

A letter exists, dated 1448, to the Bishop of Iceland
from Pope Nicholas V, lamenting the various misfortunes
that have overtaken the colonists of Greenland
to the west, many of whom then were suffering the assault

of Arctic nomads. There is another letter, dated
half a century later, in which Alexander VI observes
there has been no priest resident in Greenland
for eighty years, and Christianity is all but perished
from that frontier. Now, of this settlement,
whether it was at that time prospering, or its people
dead, little else has been recorded until the 18th
century, when a Norwegian missionary found the ruins of
a church, and the crumbled walls of several houses.
But of the Northmen themselves there was no sign.
Fur-clad Esquimaux this missionary questioned,
describing for them his multivocal rites, knew
nothing of foreign settlers or of such a religion.
Contraries happen alike to pious and to the impious.

Failure does not concern me; the condition of life
is defeat.

Pass by that which you cannot love.

He governs life who has bound the Sea,
and bridled and fettered the dark Flood.

We have found a vessel lined with moss and juniper bush,
with a burial chamber built of oak planks rammed into
blue clay beside the rail. A man was buried here
we know; we have found traces of rust from the handle
of a long-vanished sword, the head of his spear
and a shield boss, together with the charred bones of a
dog, and remnants of a horse which was buried standing.
We have found, too, six glass beads and tangled cloth,
and bits of wood carved ornamentally in high relief,
inter alia, with figures, by which we have concluded
that these people, whoever they were, held in high regard
the verity of human existence.

We found, too, the burial site of a medieval bishop
who lay on his back, hands clasped at his waist.
Thin snow drifted down the granite steps, piercing winds
tugged at the rigid yellow parchment; and we
have every reason to believe this man was interred
on the day when Timur Leng returned to Samarkand!

I am tired and discouraged. Everything
I could do, I have done.
Is it worthwhile to try again?

Je suis . . .

Someone is embracing me!

I have been alone since yesterday. If only the wind
would cease!

Did a woman speak?

Aubade?

On a plaque somewhere you will read
this inscription:
Is nothing written?
At times,
said Azeddin El Mocadecci,
we look to the end of the tale
that there should be marriage feasts
and find only, as it were,
black marigolds and a silence.

Do all rivers flow east?
And do old leaves scatter on the mountain?

Five in the morning. We lie in utter darkness.
There is no breeze. Somewhere
a man is groaning, as though he has been seized by
a hideous cockatrice, or goatish dwarf.
Are we not similar to those amphiscians
whose shadows fall at one season to the north,
but at another to the south?

Ghostly ribbons of light emerge;
I discern the placid surface of the Inland Sea.
Calm and strange
like a benediction the water slopes away.

The moon is down.

I have watched the eels
as they leave—turning, gliding without a sound,
seeking they know not what,
no more than I. But I must go
with them.

I have been studying old maps with names that trouble me
like fluttering moths—Nicobat, Penju
and Lombok, Ayuttha! I cannot wait much longer!

The tide is high.
All is possible to those who believe.

I remember a little girl dancing,
remote and untouchable,
on the bank of a river. All unknowing, she danced
the eternal promise of Womankind,
they who are
softer than boiled rice, more firm than
lemons in the spring!

She noticed me
and frowned, and went on dancing.

Cipango of glittering gems! Rich
icy silks
from Samarkand!
Nutmeg
from Malabar! Sandalwood
burns in Java!

I have walked down to the shore.
Mist covers the rice fields,
bamboo no longer rustles in the west wind.
I hear pagoda bells.

The night is brilliant; soon
it will be dawn;
the ship's bell echoes
from the furthest points of
Scorpio and Boötes.

Poise
and counterpoise.

I feel I have withdrawn and am immured,
listening. I am no different than a lens of reddest glass,
opening always to red rays,
excluding others.

Once more we are near the Cape,
the sea runs against us
and our sail is badly torn. I have inquired
of everyone, of each sailor,
what is to become of us.
They have told me, every one, the same.

The vertical rays of the sun
spell Death. This is plausible. It may be, I
do not know. But still,
my question never quite is answered.

Am I awake,
or . . .

Someone enters with clasped hands, praying aloud,
somberly, who wears a shining brocaded chasuble
that extends majestically from his shoulders
to his knees. His words reverberate from painted walls.
On a stark, wheeled table several implements
have been meticulously arranged. We who visit
are mute with anticipation. Suddenly, at a signal,
a narrow door is flung open and we witness a stranger
carried in to us from the adjoining chamber.

In our reflections
the natural order of each determines the next;
none is more,
nor can it be less than it seems.

From whatever is known to be good, shall come
its own consequence;
Evil is born of what is evil.

Of what use are words, however fateful and oracular,
if they fail to move and horrify the listener?

Daily we observe murder, concupiscence, greed, poison
and grossness, and slaughter without astonishment.
Nevertheless, it is accepted of the moralist,
the true homilist, that he repeat himself; indeed
we expect him to reiterate whatever was said before him.

Alvarado sold his rights in the conquest of Ecuador
for a sack filled with dollars made of lead. *Lá vão os pés
onde quer o coroção.*

It is said that certain savages of the New World,
when they had been persuaded to give up their convictions,
plucked wild roses which they bound to the Crucifix
as a means of indicating their adoration.
But when the Spaniards discovered what they had done
their villages were burnt and the inhabitants massacred.
In a similar fashion, we have proceeded on our way.

Father Padilla is buried beneath the floor
of the native church at Isleta.
Each twenty years the edge of his coffin becomes visible,
having worked its way upward through the earth
to warn us, and must be buried anew.

Like smoke from the ruins
of one issue
another rises,
or swallows from their nest
enact a brief continuum.

I remember a woman of San Ildefonso,
reputed to be more than a century old, who offered me
a bowl polished with obsidian stones. I accepted
this bowl in both hands, and observed that it was uneven,
as are all things. When I had placed it down
so that it rested between us, it appeared symmetrical
and was filled with beauty.

Recently, in the Mimbres mountains of New Mexico
a sheepherder who sat down to rest under a cottonwood tree
discovered a length of metal protruding from the roots.

He dug it out and found it was the hilt of a sword,
which had an elaborate basket and a marvelous arabesque
inlaid with gold; and the blade was of Toledo steel.
Now, what he did with this sword I do not know,
but it had lain three centuries beneath the cottonwood
since El Dorado passed that way.

Men hunt and fight; women dream and contrive.

The wind has changed;
it is time to go.

Thirteen years since the war.
Already it is as though it never occurred.

In good time I will desecrate monuments which offend me.

I am told of the Frenchman, Bournazel,
who wore always a scarlet tunic,
until he was advised by his commander
to show greater prudence.
Reluctantly, it is said, he dressed himself
in a khaki coat, so that he was
indistinguishable from the rest,
and on that same day he was killed.
I will find more than a little profit in this.

High in the Atlas mountains
I discovered the source of a river
and followed it,
certain it would lead to the sea.
But it grew more shallow
and turned finally into the desert,
so that when I had come to the end of it
the dunes were moist,

but nothing else was there.

Between the eastern end of the Mediterranean sea
and the northern extremity of the Syrian desert
not far from Beirut, lie the ruins of
Baalbek—stones of prodigious dimensions.
In the quarry from which these stones were brought
a single block stands, measuring
fourteen by seventy feet, which weighs
fifteen hundred tons. It has been squared, as though
the masons had readied it for levitation.

New truths are not evoked by previous generations.

Uranus found in Herschel's dream
those dreams one spent
where Bohr's celestial icon
meant each dream is folded.

Cælum non animum mutant . . .

From a distance of two hundred miles we observed
the remains of trees, humans, and animals borne aloft!

We are condemned by the course of predecession
like the water of a river;
more characteristic of ourselves,
more devious and elaborate than before.

We know of no single thing which cannot be multiplied.
And all that lies beyond our grasp
is on a sudden found in bones of minor compass,
as we sift each yesterday within our own.

Flowers, coins, and stones have been conveyed

into hermetically sealed rooms.

Miraculous results have been achieved
through the simplest means:
a bottle, a prism, a lens, a fragment of paper, an apple,
and the august, etiolate skull of a sheep
high on a summer hill.

I arrange and interpret memorable items
as vipers out of necessity, by immense labor
and with difficulty, draw themselves free
from the confines of their early, narrow sac.

Clarior ex obscuro.

Ligurius is a precious stone. When the Lynx
has pissed, he covers his piss with sand.
In seven days it has set, and become the stone.

It is well known how the Crow has power
to forecast dire events,
often spying upon Man in his treachery,
and gives warning of many things which come to pass.
But it is not true
this bird is privy to the secrets of Almighty God.

The Negro when he is drowned
looks white and loses his blackness.

At the moment of death
Azrael separates the soul from the body.

Are we not singular visitors here?

I have spent all night at work on a magnetic anchor

to dredge gold from the bottom of the Breton seas.
I have reason to anticipate success; but if I should fail,
let no man forget how opulent a dream was mine.

Just now I have heard someone say that many neglect
to discover what gives them pleasure.

Nothing exists on earth, within it, or above it
which is not of service to me.
I gather, preserve, collate, and set down each, as though
all things are stamped with varying colors.

I do not reject the magical properties of gold,
which act as a cure for ossification of the heart.

I preserve and cherish the legend of Saint Germain
who also was called Count Bellamare,
Count Aymer, and Chevalier Welldon, who claimed
to be five hundred years old,
who figured in the court of Louis XIV.
Although he was investigated by the governments of
three nations, no one could establish the place
or the date of his birth,
nor was his death recorded. It is said
he never ate; whether this is true or not
there is no doubt he mixed the finest dyes,
made jewels which deceived the experts,
and drew flaws out of diamonds.
Enormous wealth was his; and though he was followed
by royal spies, none learned the source of his money.
He was not seen to age from the day of his appearance
in the year 1746 to the day he vanished
twenty years later into Russia. Moreover
he had personal knowledge of events transpiring
centuries earlier, correct in detail.

So vivid were his recollections
that whoever heard him swore he must have been present,
which was his claim. Casanova says he died at Hesse
in 1782, but I saw him in London
yesterday. He appeared no older.

If I dare to follow these thoughts
I do not know to what depths they might lead.

Who has found love twice
in a similar way?
Dictes moy ou, n'en quel pays . . .

I hear a horse's hooves clatter on the rocks
and a lady comes riding through the trees
out of a dark Merovingian forest. Behind her
on a dun-colored horse slouches a greasy female servant
dressed in stinking rags, who shows a knife at her belt
and a sullen gaze, bawling an obscene pagan song.
I bow to the lady, who smiles and offers
good day, blessing me as though I were equal.
The brown flesh of the idolatress is repugnant,
her toes grimy in the stirrup. Night falls,
snow covers the rocks, and I here meditate
whether the vile bitch has forgotten me, or not.
More than other men I am affected by what is absent.

Pass by that which you cannot love.

I think of Nicholas de Cusa
who, after great intellectual effort, confessed himself
unable to solve the coincidence of opposites.

Now, the Manichees and the Christians held
to the same conviction, that there is a conflict between

the power of Light, which represents Good,
and the power of Darkness, which is Evil.
But the Manichees held that the outcome of this struggle
was in doubt, whereas Christians
presumed there could be none, and the power of God
must triumph. And therefore it must follow,
according to the laws of human nature,
which we know to be immutable, that if it had been
the fortune of the Manichees to attract the host
of Mankind, then no Christian would have been immured.
But because it was inevitable that men should choose
Christianity, which assuages fear and offers comfort
sorely needed, it was equally necessitous
that the Manichees, when they had been defeated,
should be slain, their corpses kicked and spat upon.

It is said of Kubilai Khan that he respected
the principal feasts of Jews,
Saracens, Idolators, and Christians.
Being asked why this was so, he replied:
There are four prophets to whom the world does honor.
Christians say their god is Jesus Christ.
Saracens venerate Mahomet.
Jews revere Moses.
Idolators pray to Sakyamuni Burkhan.
I honor each, thus I am sure to honor him who is true.
And to him I pray.

I will pray without cessation.
My faith is as pure as a hammer. Neither rock
nor brick can burn; and therefore
the earth will not dissolve in fire, as was foretold.

I believe King Arthur has come again. A fisherman
from Devon has seen the print of Arthur's men

on British sand. I believe he has come to hunt
the mighty boar, whose name is Troit,
for I have heard the terrible voice of Cabal
and saw him on a stone near Builth.

We know that many ways lead out of the King's court
and Geraint has taken a ridge from the Usk to Cardiff,
while others choose dark valleys, or go into the woods
by the river of Death. There are walls and towers, hills
and plains; these you must find both here and in Hell.

Where are the bones of Weland?
Have we more than we were given?

Wrth ein ffrwythau
yn
hadna
bydder!

Breakers, cliffs, frost, hail, gannet,
and sea-gull. I have gone past the walls
of Balclutha and they were desolate.

Waves break with the noise of avalanches across the shore
and I am far from home. Before dusk I will climb up
into the castellated cliff, there concealing myself.
Gannet and tern shall descend around me.

Arbitrarily we circumscribe reality, choosing to limit
the universe to the bounds of our apprehension.

Meanings elude all save the most acute; peripheral visions
burn undiminished past every vicissitude.

Someone has slid open the aperture of a lantern;

I see within the light
by which our multitude of shadows dance.

Who would show colors to the blind?
I abandon myself to further contemplation.

There are reports of a prodigious island in the Atlantic
to the west of Ireland, which is called Brazil.

Dawn,
chill and gray as porcelain.
I am alone.

Let them indulge their pride
if thinking I am destroyed is comfort to them;
let it be.

Men congregate in the fashion of animals
but recover their senses slowly, one by one.

No living thing is responsible for its actions.
A woman or a man is no better or worse than a stone
which, when it has been impelled in a direction,
must continue traveling until its force is overcome
and subdued by another. Not one of us prohibits himself,
nor can ever outspeed that which is responsible for us.

What is true of Alexander and Cagliostro
is true of me.

I do not know how long I have been here;
I no longer place sticks in a row;
there is no use. The day is freezing cold.
Void of hope I continue.

The assumption is made that God possesses an infinity
out of which to select for the purposes of Creation;
and that, because He is God, what He has chosen
is whatever is most perfect and must achieve
the utmost diversity of content arranged in the highest
significance; but yet some factors of the present
imply with increasing certitude a maleficence of design.
Therefore, we suspect the essential nature of God is evil.

For a little while we exist
in a world we fail to understand; every scheme
results in chaos and utmost discrepancy.

A Thorn-apple will set men dancing, allowing them
horrors of which they have neither consciousness nor
later recollection.

The Mandragora torn up by its roots
at the base of a gibbet
overthrows reason, changes men into beasts
and promptly sends women insane.

Out of the mouth of a slain priest,
according to an ancient manuscript,
burst a white dove!

Out of ashes, voices speak.

Soon we must learn the truth
that has waited in cities we have ruined.

Heaven has grown empty,
a memory of things that were, and secret unrest
gnaws a bitter taste
at the lactescent roots of being.

In each of us another lives, that we may never know.

My hair had grown long when I returned from the war.
I was wearing a padded cotton jacket and was relieved
to see our homeland. My cap was in my pocket,
friends were with me when I descended from the ship.
We were met at the gate by an old man
not one of us had ever seen, who was the age of my father,
wearing a tattered suit, who held up a colored drawing
of a soldier but did not speak. I knew at once
this must be his son, from whom he had heard
nothing. I looked at the picture, which resembled
me, with a long hooked nose and brilliant eyes.
He wore a jacket like mine, and a cap, and a black cross
adorned his breast, which I have also. I have seen
enough dead soldiers with bloated faces, green and
thick with ravening flies; for all I know,
I might have stepped on this one's belly
in my efforts to escape. I shook my head.
He stepped aside and my friends and I walked on.
But I turned to see him holding up his picture
to the millions who hurried after us.

According to Schiller, the gods of vengeance
proceed in silence.

What we have been
we remain.
Du bist
am Ende was du bist.

My brother told me once that each time
someone looked at him,
so that he longed to remain,
in that same instant was he compelled

to resume his wandering.
So was he afflicted
for jostling Christ on the road to Golgotha.

The fixed verities, constant integers of natural law,
are lessons which have escaped this world.
What is given us at birth,
the discernment of suffering,
is that sympathy which mutely atrophies.

Colonists of New England,
when they had defeated the savages,
chopped off the head of Philip
and mutilated the body,
mounting his head on a high pole
in the town of Plymouth
as a symbol of triumph, to exemplify
the course of civilization.

To think deeply right now would terrify me.

I will comfort myself with the prophecy of Seneca:
A time must come when the ocean will loosen the bonds
by which things are encircled, when the immense earth
will be revealed, when Tethys will discover the universe
anew, and Thule be no longer the end of the world.

In his own way each supplicant unites his prayer
with those of others.
Voices raised in a multitude of accents
become the single invocation.

Voltaire protested the Lisbon earthquake of 1775.
Ancient Gauls unleashed their arrows against the sky.

There was once a king of the Franks
whose name was Gunthram, who went hunting in the forest
and was overcome with sleep and laid down his head
upon the knees of his retainer. While he slept
a lizard came slithering out of his mouth
and looked for a way to cross a stream that was nearby.
Now, the king's retainer, when he saw this,
laid the king's sword across the stream
and the lizard ran across the sword and disappeared
into a hole in the hillside opposite.
And when Gunthram the king awoke he told of a vision,
vowing he had crossed an iron bridge
which spanned a mighty river and had entered a mountain
that was filled with gold. Then the king's retainer
told the king what he had seen while the king slept.
And a search was ordered and gold discovered in the hill.
Then Gunthram the king had a paten made
and adorned with precious gems
which he meant to convey to the Holy Sepulcher
in Jerusalem. But he was prevented.
You will see it on the shrine of Saint Marcellus
at Chalons, which is the capital of the kingdom
of Gunthram. And it is there to this day.

Omens, dreams, and presentiments belong to us
who are not kings, but vatic priests.

If fortune favors me, I shall discover things
so grand my name may never be forgotten
until gnomic words do not record how sorrows end.

Time was.
Time is.
Time will be.

According to Carpokrates
we are delivered from no sin we have not committed.

We know that those things which most profoundly
and most permanently affect us
have come not out of deliberate calculation,
however intricate or stupefying to the brain,
but through labyrinths of feeling
whose multiple entrances tend to elude detection;
which only much later, if at all, can be admitted.
No man likes the deep purposes of his nature
held up to study.

I proceed without confidence;
I am sick with hesitation.

Yesterday someone mentioned animals
and things sensed in darkness, and told me
a man's work should have the feel of a carving
in oak. If, he explained, it is meant to endure
and retain some characteristic meaningful
to future generations, it must at every cost
give evidence of the passage of time,
of meditation, and of skill in excess of mere
dextrous facility. Having said this, he paused;
I supposed he had concluded. Then he said
an heraldic device is not easily chiseled.

Every skilled man is to be trusted with his art.
Cuilibet in arte sua perito credendum est.

I know what I cannot prove, by reason or experiment.

It was three minutes after ten, precisely,
when he was brought to us.

He seated himself, almost indolently,
and gazed above our heads
as though relieved the time had come!
We have discussed this privately,
remembering, first of all,
that he selected a lavish supper,
that he played at cards
and joked with the Jesuit,
and toward four o'clock in the morning
lay down on the simple bed and wept,
meanwhile looking blindly all around
and through the light we kept
burning by the Governor's order.
It was then he fell asleep for the first time
in several days, and appeared to dream:
a curious expression played across his features.
And once he lifted up his hand, as though in greeting.
When he awoke and realized the hour
he seemed surprised, somehow embittered;
but then, glancing toward us
he smiled a trifle foolishly, and bent his head.
We have prayed for him, more than once. Now
who prays for us?

I do not think I soon will forget
how his hands drew suddenly up into fists, dancing
of their own accord across the polished oak arms
of the ponderous chair. I do not believe
I ever saw his face, concealed by his painted yellow
leather mask. Smoke was ascending from two holes
bored in the metal cap. For an instant
he tried to speak; and we have talked of this
between ourselves. We are of the opinion
he meant to tell us something. We think this may be so,
yet there are few things of which we can be sure.

Mon frère, a-t-il . . .

Together we are devoid of responsibility
and know no fear.

Tomorrow we must believe, if not today;
the hands of every clock are turning.

The sky is overcast.
Bluish sunlight filters down
crooked, granular, medieval streets;
and I sense a delphic voice
through the firmament of nether space.
In my heart there is no doubt
of plenary and miraculous powers.

I must establish beyond doubt the purity of my intent.

There are seven days to the week
because there are seven celestial bodies wandering
across the firmament, which are the sun and
the moon and the five planets, Mars, Mercury,
Jupiter, Venus, and Saturn. This is the reason
we call the latter days of our week
mardi, mercredi, jeudi, vendredi and *samedi.*

Two hundred years ago a certain French astronomer
observed and recorded, during the nights of May 8th
and 10th, the position of what he took to be a star.
Because these two positions failed to agree
he concluded he was mistaken and had made some error,
whereupon he continued with such matters as seemed to him
of greater magnitude, and never knew he had fixed
the planet Neptune.

As a result of multiple calculations
one faint point of light, of the fifteenth magnitude,
ultimately was discovered, whose shift in position
during a period of six days was appropriate to an object
theorized to exist in an orbit one billion miles
beyond that of Neptune. This object
was accorded the name Pluto, and its mass determined
from the perturbations of Neptune's orbit,
in natural conjunction with precursive data
which had been compiled over a number of years.
Even so, although we may describe its several properties,
predict its course, or announce its phenomenal
history, it will remain altogether as it was,
betraying itself minutely to the strongest of our senses.

Whatever occurs in the world is in accordance
with laws of perpetual truth, geometrical or metaphysical.

We understand that the supernova,
kindling a light brighter than one hundred million suns,
occurs to our knowledge each three centuries or so.
Now, three and one-half centuries have elapsed
since Kepler's phenomenon horrified the world;
and therefore we have every right to believe
our heavens will be set ablaze
more strangely than the apparition born one August morning
of secular winds across Japan.

The Roman theologian and Master of the Palace,
Spina, inquiring as to why God should permit
the death of innocents, responds in this way:
If they die not by reason of their own sins,
yet are they guilty by virtue of original sin.
Thus, it is implicit that no judge commits injustice,

since the accused cannot possibly be innocent;
and therefore whoever undertakes to defend himself
should be considered twice guilty.

Truth is not a sequence of facts;
we may be instructed by a dead man's garden.

I remember Maidanek, Davao,
and Bataan.
I could remember more;
let no man, ever, be mistaken.

Jura naturæ sunt immutabilia.
Immutable indeed are the laws of nature.

There is reputed to be a stupendous fossil which has
a quadruple bank of osseous protuberances
springing from the base of its skull.
The tail of this creature is heavily spiked
and armored, and its teeth are those of a carnivore.
Although its flesh and entrails do not exist,
paleontologists have calculated its weight,
and the dimensions of its organs, and tell us
its brain must have been approximately the size of
an infant's fist. Who reads a moral in this?

I shall continue to occupy myself with meanings that lie
beneath the surface,
in lieu of the visible prospect.

I mention at this point the log of the Yankee whaler
Monongahela, together with the testimony of
her captain, Jason Seabury, and of the men who sighted
and chased and struck with two harpoons
a plesiosaur that had survived from the Jurassic era.

These sailors measured the carcass,
finding it to be one hundred and three feet in length,
and seven inches; after which they stripped off
its meat and saved its oil, bringing this to port
to sell, because they were practical men.
Numerous sermons could abide in this.

Beyond the possibility of questioning,
certain marine reptiles once thought to be extinct
continue to live in the depths.
Through the ages they have evolved
and adapted to fantastic pressures that play upon them;
for which reason we observe them but rarely—
when they are sick, or have been injured.
On such occasions they swim toward the surface,
becoming visible to us for a little while.

I believe the sea is preparing specific revelations
for the benefit of Man,
who has forgotten the value of himself.

Now, another day comes quietly to its end.

The night is lambent;
it is wholly beautiful.

If our sun were situated at the heart of the great star
Betelgeuse,
earth's orbit would be enclosed
utterly within the shell of this superb creation.

Who knows whether we lie asleep
or a world is dreaming?

Moments alter

like this glove a woman abandoned,
expecting me to find it
hours ago; it is
somehow different than when she was here.

I remember a woman who asked me to bring my mother's heart
for her dog to eat;
and while I was carrying it
I stumbled and fell, and the heart
as it rolled in the dust
cried out: *T'es tu fais mal, mon enfant? T'es tu*
fais mal?

Thoughts of women—brutal, obscene fantasies—
obsess and torture me.

I was ill and thought I would die,
and spoke to the woman I loved. She listened
while covering her head with a scarf.

Women are suspicious of men that explore the depths.
Women feel a brooding affinity with water.
I understand, as I contain their nature within my own.

I am told of structures that have no windows
but only narrow slits, by means of which
a man may defend himself and his family.
On top of these buildings there is a flat roof
with a parapet around, over which the women
always are visible, peeping down at the struggle
while they contemplate who shall come up to them
when it has ended. The difference, they feel,
is small; women respect the victor.

Rabovsky materializes in the dreams of women;

he is the fabled incubus, which is their one desire.

I hear someone coughing; a noise
like dry reeds splintering. I turn in time to see
someone lean forward, coughing again
and again; and it seems I have fallen
steeply through one experience into another,
into a chthonic world where
I am lulled by strange expectancies.

I hear the rushing noise of space, the unmistakable sound
of our journeying earth; and I behold a woman
dressed all in black, whose lace gloves
reach to her elbows. Out of her bodice the nipples
of her bosom spring like blossoms from Japan,
or the pink sockets of the blind. By gaslight her thighs,
murky and evil as twin serpents, openly invite me.
She smiles and beckons; but I notice another man
seating himself in the shadows,
who regards me with amusement. At this instant
three solemn raps are heard, the green flames shrink,
and I depart the theater in great haste, remembering
I have seen his face before. Tonight I leave;
I set sail at once toward the holy city which they call
Byzantium. But yet I know we three will be aboard.
Plus ça change, plus c'est la même.

When once we know them, symbols lose their magic.

This morning there was no sunrise.
Rain struck ominously against the gelid glass.

I could, if I chose, remember much: scenes, words
and strains of music, phrases from Vinteuil
we seal like ferns in sediment—bleak Assyrian pictures

there is little need to draw again.

Is it my self that speaks,
or through me the spirit of an age?

To the moral man
nothing takes root less deeply in the soul
than Jesuitic attitudes;
and therefore we seldom should wonder if
a majority of lives are spent
in useless answers.

Moralities are built of transitory things.
Who loves twice in a similar way?

I do not know how long it has been since anyone
reached out to me. When I was young
I thought I could not live without love;
but I am older now, sifting and weighing
motes of dust.

There will be a time, someone told me,
when you know that spring is near,
when snows melt in the field
and a moment for which you have lived
is come round at last.

Verweile doch, du bist so schön.
Linger awhile, thou art
so fair.

I believe in the curative properties of silver;
I set twin florins on my eyes when I am tired.
I think a chestnut in a leather bag is good
to ward off evil. I empty out of my pockets

each charm and relic my wife has secreted there,
yet my love for her is both positive and constant.

My brother just this instant has remarked that
into every woman he meets he projects whatever
of himself is base. Yet there is nothing that is base
in any man, not more than in a woman. We live as we must.
Still, each time I gaze at my brother's visage—
at his brutal, shapeless lips—I cannot be certain.

There are few things about which we may be positive
in regard to women, but it is well known
that amongst them the seat of wantonness is the navel.

I feel obligated to comment on the woman of Italy
whose body was surrounded by a halo of light.
Unquestionably she entertained profound ideas
on the nature of religion, and we suppose
deep changes occurred within her. I would say
the stringency of her Lenten fast may have resulted
in an excess of sulphides which became excited by
certain ultra-violet radiations inherent in the blood.
I believe, as is evident, in miracles; I believe also
in the values of science.

What first existed was born in robes of phantasy.

No count was possible at Hiroshima; consider the centuries
and keep silent.

Oracular calculations demonstrate it may be possible
to eradicate terrestrial life. A certain biophysicist
posits one unique explosive object to the weight of
ten thousand tons, which, under optimum conditions,
should produce sufficient dust to poison the atmosphere

so that nothing could survive. However, preliminary
studies undertaken by one government institute suggest
that the manufacture of such an agent might necessitate
a total effort of at least eight years and would cost
approximately forty billion dollars; and, even so,
there could be not the slightest guarantee of success.

By how much is any man more consequential than I, or I
than he, or we both than some other, or again, he than us
both; by so utter a margin is that superior where nominal
expectations fail less often.

There can be no doubt that one essential precondition
of intuitive thinking is the exclusion of rational
or factual considerations; Kekule solved the problem
of the benzene molecule during a fatigue-engendered dream
when he beheld a viper swallowing its tail.

Now this day, too, has ended.
The world may look the same, but is not.

It is enough at this point to say
the Wolf invariably is born during the first thunder
of May, which means the Devil was thrown down
from Heaven in his first Pride.
I think this is so, but I am not sure.

To become a man is the greatest art.

Marco Polo relates that hawks belonging to Kubilai Khan
wore silver tablets attached to their feet.
Now, silver does not corrode, and many hawks
when they had been released, never were seen again.
I believe that if I search the Mongol empire

from one end to its other, undissuaded in my quest
by thoughts of profit, lascivious women, or
inclement weather, I will find in the forest
or upon the steppe a regal silver tablet inscribed:
You hold on your wrist the hawk of Kubilai Khan!

Soon, I think, I will come to the river
of Kara-moran which flows through the mighty lands of
Prester John, who, it is said,
conversed with Jews in the north of Asia
that never had heard of the siege of Jerusalem
nor of Jesus, nor of our Redemption!

There lived at one time in the city of Mien
a very rich king, who, when it came his turn to die,
commanded that two towers be erected over his tomb,
one of gold and the other of silver. He ordered
their shape to be circular, and all around them
thousands of gilded bells should be hung.
Last night, just as the moon was rising,
a breeze blew into our encampment and we heard
a tinkling noise. The tomb of this king
must be nearer to us now than ever before.

It is known that while quantities of Chinese silk
were passing by way of caravan into the Roman empire
the Romans had no idea from whence such luxuries came;
and not until seven hundred years after Jesus Christ
did Europe first suspect the existence of a civilization
other than its own. Now, we again suspect what long
has been. And what is left to come subtly may prove
our last estate; so madness plots the route of caravans.

Idly we comfort ourselves; what will be

has been foretold.

We live in the final tepid rays of the Christian era.

The green gum of frankincense smoldered ominously
on early altars when Legions rowed
to England.

Designs which exceed our comprehension are summoned
for their purpose.

Phantoms outbalance the conscious mind.

It is rumored that among certain papers in the Vatican
are clues relative to the fate of the Greenland colony
which mysteriously disappeared five centuries ago.
No one has explained why these papers have so long lain
undisturbed within the archives. Might it not be that
memories of our failure wheel over us, more pitiless
and unremorseful than Enguerrand's falcon?

Pius V, in conference with his advisers,
all at once stopped speaking and held up his hand.
Without a word he hurried to the nearest window,
where he remained with a look of absolute concentration.
Turning at last to his advisers, who had waited
uneasily, perplexed and astonished, he told them
of a marvelous victory which had been scored
in the name of Christendom. Later came news of Lepanto,
where, during those same moments, the course of battle
changed—the Turks were repulsed, and Europe saved.
We are overcome with unspeakable awe in the fabric of
miracles.

Poincaré conceived of unimagined dimensions,

of five and six.

From the age of twenty Agrippa conducted experiments
in chrysopœia.

We are at rest in the center of the universe
and are encircled by the course of the sun
that shines upon us and solicitously bestows
its warmth. Thus, we prepare for eternal life.

The star Epsilon Aurigæ, whose position is calculated
some 3° from Capella, is partially eclipsed
each twenty-seven years by a fantastic object
no astronomer has yet seen. Across the penultimate
reaches of the universe there is nothing
half so terrible as this. My faith is like a hammer,
but I am stupefied with dread.

We are the Dioscuri,
and one is mortal.

In order to appreciate those qualities
which are most valuable and original,
the beauty and power of which is no other's,
we should know to what extent and from whom
the transference has been effected.
Concerning choice, disposition, embellishment, and style
we need to inform ourselves quite thoroughly.
If, let us say, some liturgical topic
has been appointed to a man's particular usage,
wherewith he has so played across it
that it appears to alter before our eyes
like the features of a familiar statue
struck with firelight, until we grow bemused
and silent, half-convinced this lifeless object

may turn toward us to speak, or to enfold us
in a marble grasp, censure proves its own conceit.
Cuilibet in arte sua perito credendum est.

During the 18th century there was a woman,
supposedly mute, who was conducted about the countryside
by ecclesiastics; and, at every stop they made,
in every wayside chapel, she was seen miraculously
to recover the power of speech. We believe as we wish.

I have heard of a man who, when he lay dying,
realized that in the house adjoining his own
a suicide was imminent; whereupon, with an expression of
desperate haste, he lifted himself from his deathbed
and staggered into the house of his neighbor
where the suicide was dangling from a beam, and
swiftly cut the rope, to the amazement and terror of
those that followed. Mine, also, is a presentiment
of incomprehensible events.

Vortices exist through which a man may be abducted.

I have torn to pieces
the plans with which I had been provided.

I cannot forget the estuary brimming with corpses,
nor the exotic flowers.

Du bist am Ende was du bist.
I choose to teach the infinitude of Man.

The Luciferians, a sect which flourished during
the 14th century, listing numerous adherents
among the mendicant orders, had no doubt God seized
the throne of Heaven by force, treachery, and usurpation.

I have fixed my lens.
Now I will wait; there is time enough. Soon
I must perceive the first point
of color,
followed by a thread of rising smoke.
God give me to say what I have suffered.

Evil shall be believed
when it rides home to stare at us.

Lat. 30.48 S.; Long. 92.10 E.
The focus alters.
Whosoever my brother is, I would not play false to him.

Of those multitudes which have passed before us,
few appear deserving of our notice;
and yet we should recall how equivalently
we soon shall be lost among future throngs,
and that eye now turned round upon us
quickly enough shall turn back once again.
Our utmost hope, therefore, should be no less
than to assuage the traveler in his extremity,
trusting we go not unregretted.

We are informed by M. Sainte-Beuve
how the very greatest names are those which distress
or swing counter to every fixed belief.

It is well known how Alexander Pope
affixed to Bolingbroke's letter to Swift
a terse note to the effect
that some advantage to their age might accrue,
should they spend three years together.
I will meditate further on this.

I have thought of Ruskin as an old, demented man

with emptied eyes and the beard of a river god,
seated in his favorite chair. If a polished pebble,
a coin, a picture, or any object that he had loved
were placed in his hand, he would smile. Or if
Severn children petted him. But like a young and
weary child himself, the scalloped mind hung dangling.
Seldom did he notice much, outside his endless dream.

There is much that we know in regard to corporeal objects,
but less in regard to the human mind, and still less
of our earliest beginnings—the God of Asine and Tænarum
walked on water long before the birth of Jesus.

My brother, who is a teacher, although few can discover
what it is he teaches, spoke this morning of capacities,
of how we tend to hold in mind particular aspects
and properties we deem attractive; and, comparing,
contrive those recondite associations, perform and think
through symbols, pretend, and remove ourselves out of
each world into another. I will ask him if I am, in fact,
a marvelous creation. I doubt he will answer; there is
not a sound, except the scratch of his pen across paper.

Those which are disparate, so as to be bound
in opposition, necessarily unite with each other
by virtue of inverse conjunction.

A fish that lives in the deep gloom of a cavern
will grope toward the light, if it can see or
otherwise sense the brilliance of the outer world.
Whether or not it shall perish in this unaccustomed
glory, still it has removed itself from the company
of its fellows. And always those which remain
are those with little sensitivity to light—the blind

that beget the blind. This is a parable of our time.

Night. I am alone. I will allow nothing
to interrupt the course of hariolate cogitation.

A voice has told me that before this journey ends
I shall see the drowned Phœnician sailor.

Someone just now has proposed that civilization
must endure successive cycles
of evolution and self-destruction!

The Governor has advised us to prepare ourselves
in such a manner as to seem
neither sumptuous and hedonistic, nor
unnecessarily ascetic. Perhaps we are not unlike children
shut off in the narrowest room of a moldering castle,
surrounded by a deep, impenetrable forest,
who, because they perceive nothing,
are doomed to live in utter ignorance of the extent
and boundaries of their true domain.

Pennies are placed upon our eyes.
Coins of Ampuria and Rhoda are found in Gaul.

We alone have constituted authority over time.

A substance can begin only after it has been created,
and cease not until it has been annihilated.

What should I say next?

The clouds must be warm and low, which means
someone will visit me when I least expect.

I have walked carefully to the door
and stand beside it, my hand poised above the latch.

This shall prove our season of excitement
when coruscate madness blinds us; together we stoop
and recover our senses, slowly,
one by one.

Mambres and Jannes brought up frogs
into the land of Egypt, but could not get them out.

Mumphazard was hanged because he would not speak.

I am ill. Someone has touched me;
I need to lie down.
I would scatter dots on a sheet of paper, or practice
the art of geomancy,
if that would be enough.

Ice floats on the water! This means our lives
are pledged.
Honor is at stake.

We know of a ruin called Ys
at the bottom of the Breton seas. Fourteen days ago
we drifted over it,
where it lies, fanciful and green. But now
sluggish waves break and foam about us;
the wind is bitter, it blows from the north.
The door to the chartroom is locked,
and there is no sound within.

Late this afternoon a monstrous creature
appeared out of the fog, its body scarcely rippling
the Arctic tide, its head swaying, lowering

and rising high above us
as though these present hours still were Jurassic,
and this ship and all of us on board
were spending eternity in nacreous waters.
Nota habeat ea signa quibus obsess . . .

On the crest of a phosphorescent wave
I see the figurehead of a Viking longboat!

I am deeply troubled.

On Kingigtorsuak Island we discovered
three cairns, and a stone
which bore this inscription:
Erling Sigvatsson and
Bjarne Thordarson and
Endride Oddson raised
these cairns Saturday
before Rogation Day.
But this is all we understood,
because there followed
six terrifying symbols
none of us ever had seen.

By our fruit
are we known.

Painted on the wall of a passageway in the cathedral
at Schleswig are eight turkey cocks!
These paintings date from the time the cathedral was built
in the year 1280. Historians claim
there were no turkey cocks in Europe until
Spaniards brought them back from Mexico.
Now, the Greenland hunters admired the polar bear
and the falcon, sending home specimens from the New World,

and no one denies the existence of white hunters
on the mainland of America long before the birth of
Susanna Fontanarossa.
From this we draw our own conclusion.

There can be no doubt of cosmos within chaos,
order among disorder,
and a law to each contingency.

During a battle between Norsemen and savages
a woman whose name was Freydis
picked up the sword of her husband, who had been slain,
and as the Esquimaux rushed toward her
she drew out her breasts and slapped them
with the blade. The savages were appalled;
they dropped their weapons and fled.
This woman's act may be understood by
women of every age, but not by any man.

The cave is not at rest until it is entered.
Purple and ermine are the colors of women,
and their wound.

We know that when a man bows down he modifies himself
and becomes a servant, who says:
The sight of you brings me such pleasure
that I take my ease. But soon I must rise again,
for the thought of further pleasure possesses me.
When a woman curtsies, we know she is saying:
Because I see you, resistance vanishes.

It is late.
A clock chimes.

I have lost all sense of existence.

The wind blows from the east at five knots.
Pelicans coast on the water.
We are close to land.

The sky is overcast
and the date I set down
is the 13th of April.
The year is 1886. Tomorrow
I become twenty years of age.
I am well and look forward to life,
but also I am able to look into the past.

It was the 19th of May in 1845
when the two ships of Sir John Franklin's expedition
last were seen. Searchers discovered
only a scrap of paper revealing that Franklin had died,
the ships had been abandoned, and survivors
were starting across the ice.
Six years later the crew of a British merchantman
met two ships riding high above the water
on an iceberg of fantastic dimensions.
The admiralty description of Franklin's ships
matches the description of these spectral vessels
coursing polar seas, whose name are *Erebus*
and *Terror*.

It is known that ships at sea develop a psychic entity;
and this is why the foundering of a ship
fills the beholder with awe. Whoever speaks
while his ship slides into the ocean will be damned
throughout all eternity.

Lat. 70.10 N.; Long. 12.18 W.
I hear the sound of a reef.
Others have heard it, too—I am certain

because not one man has mentioned it!

I have just this instant seen a face in the mirror
and observed its moving lips, which seemed to say that
I no longer am where I was; I shall be found
not in Sicily nor Edinburgh, but where I least anticipate,
and thou also.

I have had experiences no one would credit.
I might compose a letter concerning them,
which would be read with great eagerness, if only
I conjecture to whom it should be addressed.

Another flake has fallen through the years.

These moments evolve bright with detail;
each I must study as meticulously
as though it were the vein of a leaf. None
should leave me less. If I am rich
with borrowed excellence, yet am I rich. Is this
not better than to be impoverished?

Since noon I have waited beside the sea wall.
Idly a young girl is approaching,
dressed in a robe of blue English brocade.
It is August in Brittany. The sun beats down
on metallic waves. Suddenly I realize
this coast has been deserted for centuries
and I am not myself, but the embodiment of all men
in whose sight she is without Evil, full of Grace.
How should I surpass what I behold?
Now, who am I? Tell me, if you are able.

Regret is useless;
rivers flow down to the sea.

Since dawn I have watched boats in the harbor.
Plus ça change, plus c'est la même.

Those aspects of the human body most highly esteemed
by earlier ages seem nugatory to this time:
old, old drawings of the foot look wooden and sheer.
Centers of absorption pass. By those who understand,
seldom are interpretations asked, or given.

I have come upon the print of a woman's foot in
deliquescent sand. Her name, which she had traced with
a stick, embellishing it with fluted shells,
has not yet been washed from sight.
How should I contrive a symbol that befits her,
so that no man, seeing it, can forget?
Aut inveniam aut faciam. Before the moon rises
I must find a way.

As Thou to Me, so
I
to Thee.

I have set my wages on the Wheel of Fortune
again. Again, the arrow
hesitated, but moved on. Tomorrow
I will succeed.

How shall we redeem all we have lost?

Is Man destined to remain an actor
and a Pharisee?

The celebrated star of Tycho Brahe
first was observed on the 11th day of November
in the year 1572, not long after the massacre

named for Saint Bartholomew, who was flayed alive
and hung, head downward, for his belief.
Thirty thousands were cruelly slaughtered
by order of Catherine de Medicis, the Duke of Anjou,
and others. Astrologers proclaimed the Star of Bethlehem
had come to announce the end of the world.
But when seventeen months had gone
the star of Brahe dimmed and was not seen again;
nor any disaster fell, save what was occasioned
by human fright and folly.

The cinders of a city have written
smokily against wall: *Thou art . . .*

It is time to be exact. According to Thomas Browne,
being ignorant of evils to come, or forgetful
of evils past, is a merciful provision of Nature
whereby we digest the mixtures of our few days, and,
our delivered senses not relapsing into remembrance,
our sorrows are not thus kept alive and raw
through the chancre of needless repetition. Yet
I would say that as we so entrust this present state,
few shall mark the diligence of our journey's end,
white with ashes.

After the *Enola Gay* completed its flight
rape, robbery, and murder became not uncommon.
Schoolgirls turned willingly into whores
and their brothers grew into thieves. Despair
and hunger drove them, but also the appeal of chaos.
Later, it is said, these strangely experienced children
spoke with nostalgia of that time, just as
the shore becomes visible after its highest tide.

I was walking with my son in the direction of the estuary

where I meant to explain, as best I could,
the genesis of those incalculable conditions
which now afflict us, when we encountered a child
peeling shreds of skin from her body.
Her lips had melted, and she was blinded,
yet I think she was not unaware; it seemed to both
my son and myself that we could hear singing,
although it is possible we were somehow deceived.

Each of the world's religions has prophesied
a fiery ending to the reign of Man.

Be any man laden with sick
women, children, sisters, or domestics, or be
he ill himself,
then let them lie where they be;
and we praise him, too,
if he would burn himself, or
that feeble person.

There was a moral factor, as I am the first to admit. I
have been meaning to . . .

We recognize, of course, how the presence of
each individual augments the total preparation;
during the 14th century incest was permitted,
if practiced upon an altar.

Fear him who trod upon the ape and the basilisk,
who conquered the lion and the dragon!
In the year 1350 the faithful were summoned to Rome
to celebrate the Jubilee and a marked lessening
of the Plague. But with these pilgrims came the flea,
so that out of every hundred, not one survived.
This may be regarded as a significant lesson for today.

The law of non-contradiction states that any proposition
and its opposite cannot both be true, and that whatever
implies a contradiction, or offers two values negating
each other, by definition must prove unreal; from which
we distinguish truths of fact from truths of reason.

Aquinas was of the opinion God alters the universe
at His pleasure, but yet there is one restriction:
He must obey the logic of Aristotle.
He may create, however He wills, a five-tailed ass,
but always a triangle shows three angles.

How am I obligated to the logic of other men?

A small proportion of the earth bears wheat;
circles rotate of their own accord.

The Ecclesiastic has told me that because
our society is perishing,
and of this there can be no doubt,
whoever should wish to restore it must first recall
those principles out of which its strength was born.
How shall I accomplish this?

Last night, in response to my questioning,
the Astronomer paused in his work
and said that if his private wish were granted
he would extend to a trifle past infinity
the visible boundaries of our dominion.
I therefore suggested he petition
for a newer and much longer telescope.
He smiled, reminding me of how our monies
always have been allotted to a sharper purpose.
I could see that he was not embittered,
for which I was puzzled; but then,

without a word he bent to resume his study
of the Pleiades.

Encore, les extrêmes se touchent!

Strange formulæ
were requisite to medieval therapeutics.
The more revolting and grotesque the ingredients
of any potion,
so much more efficacious was it deemed.
Additional words for today.

Historians apprise us that exposure of court poisoning
did not put an end to this practice; indeed
when it became known and a punishment established
eight poisoners flourished
where one had worked before. This
I set in ecru letters, because of its importance.

Chronicles record the ecstasy of returning life
while the virulence of the Plague diminished.
There were new fashions, symbols, and ornaments;
and the allegory of color became a language
we have never lost.

At length this day, like many of hers, comes to its end.

The moving visions of Salvius, of Furseus and Drihthelm
commence in the same manner as that of Er, who lay dead
while his soul was conducted both to Hell and to Heaven.
In this way do we enter unnamed regions, while we sleep.

In the constellation of Cygnus the filamentary nebula
reaches outward a distance equivalent to
forty million times the distance of the earth
from the sun. It was in Manila a man told me this,

and as he spoke, an east wind was blowing
across Luzon. It is true, he said;
and he wore in his ear the ring that sailors fix
to show they have crossed the China Seas.

Why should I feel as desolate as I do? Is it because
our senses tell us the world is hostile,
cold, and dead? Do we count and check
the divinity that sleeps within us, and make our lives
a sum of antiquities further than Etrurian tombs?

If you disparage the Devil
you must answer to the Church.

Can you mutilate one face of a coin, yet not diminish
the value of both?

I remember a man crouching in the shadow of
a whitewashed wall, selling goods his daughter had stolen.
He saluted me in Arabic: I returned his salutation
as best I could. Then, for a little while,
we squatted in the shade and gazed at leafless
desiccated hills burning in the midday sun. Ahmed Mizal
was his name. His burnous was covered with dust.
He informed me that the earth is a night light
sunk into a cup in the mountain of Kaf. And he said:
I leave you to discover what I mean.

Wisdom is valued
at one-half the daily expense of the world.

I consider the emperor
who, each time he sat down to eat,
took from a golden chain which hung about his neck
the helix of a unicorn

and dipped this into his food.
If it grew discolored, the meal was poisoned.

It has been recorded that the Count of Vermandois,
treacherously arrested by Alexius, was taken
a close prisoner from Durazzo to Constantinople.
The reason was Alexius' terror of the Crusaders
and their implacable design. By duplicity he expected
to intimidate the hostile Christians; but in this
he was disappointed, as every man deserves to be
who engages in, or contrives, any malevolent act
for the purpose of future welfare.

I cannot imagine what to say next.

I once observed a moth fluttering blindly out of a
crevice; immediately I hurried to look at myself
in a mirror. My features expressed fright and abhorrence.
Whatever exists without the use of intellect is, to me,
terrifying and repugnant.

It is said that during an interim in the dissection of
Napoleon's body his heart was eaten by a rat.

A certain carpenter by the name of Montgomery,
having been tormented by yowling cats,
knew they could not be what they seemed
but were witches assuming this shape.
That is why he armed himself and struck at them.
Now, when two old women died and their bodies
had been laid out, various marks and scars
were observed; and, the carpenter
swearing he flogged two cats in just this way,
the people of his parish set themselves
to discover corroboration. Is it not to be expected

that presently their proof was found?

Sir Matthew Hale, addressing the jury
on an occasion which is no longer of interest to us
remarked he could not in the least doubt the existence
of sorcery, since the laws of every nation
provide against it, wherefore
it cannot fail to exist. Should this be considered
appropriate to our day?

I have been thinking for a long time
of the rector of Framlingham, in Suffolk,
who excited his neighbor's suspicions,
leading them to believe he must be a wizard;
and of how, when he had been condemned,
he begged the funeral service of his church
be read to him. Being denied,
he gave it himself out of his memory
to them, while he walked to the scaffold.

It is on account of the future I concern myself
with the past;
I cannot one-fifth articulate my passion.

Today in this austral gulf
it is hotter than anywhere I have ever been.
I lie in the shade of the sail
thinking about the summer town where I was born.
I think of my mother and of my sisters,
who do not know what has become of me.
I doubt they have heard news these past twelve years,
though someone might have told them
I was glimpsed in Maracaibo or Port Said,
assuming this should be some comfort. Or
they may well have forgotten my name,

or reply to whoever asks that I am drowned.

I am not my father's child; I have conceived
myself, out of my own sperm.
Who is not the consequence of himself?

I have just now seen the captain, who tells me
we are in search of the golden city of Manoa!
He has purchased a chart on which a cross is drawn
not far from where we lie becalmed.
But I have studied other charts, which show
nothing except the sea for a thousand leagues
in every direction. If I should make this known
he would order me to fetch the sextant,
that he might ascertain our position and alter course
if need be. Should I say to him
we have reached Manoa, and been there many years?

When shall we wake from our prodigious dream?
Auch ich war in Arkadien geboren.

It is known the Celts so hated the Saxons
that they would not attempt to convert them,
for fear they should succeed and these Saxons
be saved. What is the meaning of this?
I cannot provide a meaning; there are several.

It is further known how the rise of mendicant orders
marked the ecclesiastic expression of a resurgent people,
for which reason I am here, and you. Together we shall
form our entity, against which no power can prevail.

I have seen among figures of animals in Rhodesian
cliff dwellings a double cross within a circle,
which is called the sun-wheel, and greatly antecedes

the wheel we know; therefore the source of it
cannot have been the external world.

Gradually the future is becoming clear to me;
the future is not unlike a turbulent pool
that as it grows settled permits us to discern objects
lying on the bottom, less distorted than they were.

Because the coherence of perceived phenomena
implies the outer world, we say it is so; but yet
this neglects to answer the question of
how we establish the existence of substances
beyond these central phenomena. Each construction
of necessity embodies, in addition to its argument,
one view of the universe and the moral implications
thereof; which we find either agreeable or repugnant,
according to our nature.

Earthly bodies fall from their desire to be nearer
the center of the universe.

Alaricus turned a river
to hide his bones at the bottom.

The Dean of Saint Paul's determined to pose
for the monument which would commemorate him; he
stood upon a wooden urn wrapped in his winding sheet.

It is ourselves we love with passionate emotion;
ourselves we seek.

Au royaume des aveugles . . .

I am not able to express what I mean! Should I
from necessity begin again?

Sticks tossed in the channel are borne away.
We cannot escape, and yet
beyond doubt it is death to linger here.

Saul has this day found a bronze anchor ring
half-buried in the sand.

First New Moon of the year. The wreckage has drifted;
we could hear the surf, and by this light
distinguish a multitude of gulls
wheeling above the splintered mast. The reef is
a spectral thing rhythmically offered, open
like a woman's body and then soon concealed by
lucent, rolling waves. We are not positive where we are,
nor do we hope.

Today the water is calm.
The wind blows out of the east. In the red grotto
from whose roof depends a myriad of lobsters
like fantastic ornaments, we encountered
three sharks asleep, motionless
in a Byzantine hall. Someone murmurs
that we live not unlike these regnant, claustral beings
which swim through perpetual night.

A piece of gold has washed up on the beach!
My brother has seen it, and tells me this is an omen—
a Spanish dollar flung ashore by the drowned Commander
who wearies of his fleet where it waits
at the bottom of the Gulf; and sends for us
to raise him, with all his men,
that they may return to their wives in Spain,
toward which they set sail three centuries ago.
We have seen his flagship, *San Luis Obispo*,
in blue water; we have watched stones we dropped

come to rest against its bow,
and have seen barracuda gliding over it
and fabulous reptiles hover with mindless pleasure
through deep reaches of the sun where it lies
unspoiled, glittering among anemones.

Who can hear me? Where should I turn?

Our hands grow weary from stretching forth
and riches are everywhere, further than we can see.

On the far side of a certain lake,
not more than fifty leagues from the sea,
a volcanic mountain rises abruptly from a treeless plain.
The summit of this mountain is perpetually obscured,
except for a single hour each year
when the clouds fold apart, no man can say why.
Halfway up the eastern slope of this peak,
which is called Cheptah, lies the entrance to
a mine—the richest in the entire world,
beside which the temple of Daibaba is as nothing!
When we have come to Cheptah we will gather
nuggets of gold as large as lemons,
and twist heavy chunks of silver out of the walls
 more easily than fruit is twisted from its stem. Tomorrow
we will go, as soon as it is light.

The road from Cuzco to Mayapán is not far.

There is known to be a shallow river in which
the savages wade, carrying reed baskets;
and these they fill up with priceless treasures.
In times of drouth the bed of this river becomes visible
for a distance of one thousand miles,
so dazzling it is to the imaginations of men. Come

with us, or stay.

When at great length he had confessed
his deep obligations to our company, including
those that were absent,
for such love and loyalty to himself, as he said,
which he forever wished to honor and reward
when God should be pleased
to offer him repose from this earthly labor,
he adjured us most solemnly to pray for him
that through mercy, forgiveness, and
the prosperity of celestial beneficence
his soul might be received
in compliance with almighty rectitude.
Asking that we might relieve him of whatever sins
toward which we may have charged him
in times past, for that in such a way his pain
might be alleviated and his anxiety moderate,
he clasped both hands across ours, one
after the other, shut his eyes,
and descended into Hell. And there was none
of our company that sighed or winked
the faintest tear. We stood amazed
that any man could go to Death with such hypocrisy,
believing his deeds much other than they were.
His stinking corpse we wrapped in the blanket
of a poisoned horse and, having
weighted it with stones, by the usage of
a forked stick, without further ceremony,
rolled it to the river. It may be that none of us
shall pass this way again.

De donde vienes, amor,
mi niño?
Hast thou not ever seen the oranges of El Naranjal?

I think I have heard just now the clink of metal
and a nickering of horses—the stamp of
hooves on marshy soil. Oñate has returned
and one man is wounded: a brightly feathered arrow
adorns his throat. Beneath a cottonwood
carefully they place him down,
whose one eye is open, the other shut. Oñate
watches, but says nothing, stroking his beard.
Hours elapse. They bury him beside the stream,
his sword beside him. El Dorado waits
ten *varas* beyond the pass, and sunlight reflects
from Sevillian armor. Soon they are lost
and I hold in my hand a dollar from Madrid—
purer than Quivira will surrender,
with echoes longer than the gloomy clank of
stirrups beside the magic water.

Ay, Estevan! Ay! Ay!
Estevan! Where lies this fabled city?

If you find nothing of consequence, he said
as I was leaving, send back
a cross no longer than your hand.
But it seemed to me I could see a gilded palace
beyond the mudbrick Zuñi huts,
and one arid myth became a dream.

Appearance passes; truth abides.

One-fifth of the world's total treasure
waits to be recovered
from caverns and foundered galleons.

Once I came upon a Phœnician anchor, from which I
was able to determine that the vessel had been

a sumptuous, marvelous thing; for which reason
I followed its chain as far into the depths as I could,
and I am positive the hulk lies not much deeper; yet
our brightest torches thus far have failed to pierce
the obscurity of historic travels.

Very early I grew able to distinguish
whatever gives rise to fundamentals.
From lesser problems have I turned aside.
Little wonder men should pause as I walk by;
small wonder, indeed, they grow embittered
and resentful. Each shouts his claim, announcing
how boldly he will surpass my achievement
tomorrow. If thinking so is pleasure, I respond,
let it be. When the mouth has been opened
the soul is visible.

Without adequate knowledge of the sea and sky
we perish of spiritual hunger.

There is ambergris in the belly of the cachalot
and the whale, the two greatest of fish.

There is a plant called dittany
which, when it has been ground up and devoured,
makes a man impervious,
so he is not hurt by arrows.

I have learned that violet cures tuberculosis
and augments the sex of Man. But I cannot say
whether I am awake or sleeping.

Babylonians pictured the universe
as a circular island ringed by the sea,
with a hollow half-sphere overhead

and doors for the transit of celestial objects
east or west. Egyptians distinguished
among planets and grouped their constellations,
apprehending the universe through some other sense:
Heaven is a woman, or a beast,
the sun a God that sailed all day, and every night
came visiting the abode of the dead.
But I believe the universe must be a drifting stone
or a leaf.

The activity of that internal principle
enabling one perception to illuminate or prepare another
is known as appetition.

Lâo-Tse,
who was of supernatural conception,
was carried in his mother's body for sixty-two years.
That is why his hair was white at birth.

I believe in the immortality of life, but
at the same time I cannot quiet my longing for rebirth.

Prior to the Resurrection it is said
He descended into Hell for three full days,
whose name was Tamuz, son of Ishtar,
which means the son of God.
Is it not shameful what we see in this?—
our salvation and the renascence of the earth.

My abhorrence is stronger than death! I am
Eteocles and Polyneices burning!
The flame of my body divides in unconquerable loathing!

Last night I awoke conscious of a deadly gaze,
and knew that something had begun to settle itself on me.

I was not able to breathe; and I understood
I had been chosen to regain those occult faculties
which belonged to pre-history. Soon, I think,
objects will have lost their power to excite me.
Even now, as I consider the skin of my hand, it appears
translucent. Before much longer I shall seek refuge
in another world.

Whoever grows blind has no desire to see;
whoever's voice is lost owns a secret it fears to tell.

When we have become insolent through prosperity
and trample across the prayers of the weak,
then into our souls stalks a terrible figure,
while palaces burn.

In the year 1198 all Europe was swept with alarm
when it became known that the Antichrist had been born
in Babylon. Is there a purpose to such happenings?
Or are they but insane vicissitude ? — senseless
motions, midnight-wrought of frenetic dreams, nourished
by the breath of a cockatrice.

Who is there? Who speaks?

Death and destruction have heard the sound of wisdom,
as the pitcher has been shattered at the fountain,
and the wheel was broken by the cistern.

Forgive us, we live a lie,
monstrous
and full of iniquity.

I have lost track of time. I follow the nightwatch
and wait. Nothing ventures near this place;

even the waves retreat in anguish and horror. We
can only hope.

In the south of France there is a root known as *car*,
which for thousands of years has been used
to express whatever is barren, stony, or hostile. Now
do you understand?

I must leave no doubt of my intent.
I will repeat this prayer:
Mon frère, a-t-il . . .

Can no one accept me as I am?
Listen! — I was naked, but I felt no shame,
merely a recollection of its usage.
Yet I was not blind; I could marvel at the trees
of Nigitsu. How can I say more?

My daughter is in those ashes!
Was her life given up to some cause
you can find?

It has been gray and cold these past days,
I have been alone too much. Or it may be only that
I have looked too long through Sphinx eyes,
hoping for one glimpse of reality.
I will put aside what is extraneous
in order to continue my work. It is late and I
acknowledge the insufficiency of time.

Wind burls about the stinging rope!
The ship rolls on.
By dawn, if all goes well, we hope to raise Shinju.

At Maidanek the count was kept; at Hiroshima

all was lost.

None is born conscious of his own birth in time;
few have heard Jehovah speak.

I will go down into my self where dark seeds
lie fallow, waiting the chosen moment,
and no winds blow. Here is the place
visions wither and dreams decay, where bleak rocks
keep the date. During your last hour
do not plead, or pretend you heard no warning.

Darkly from its hidden orifice
tumultuous wells the nameless river.

I will tell you once more: the end was born
of its own beginning
when the sun shone like a ruby through the night
and crusts of ice were shattered
by mountain peaks. Are you
listening?—it is almost midnight. This may be
our last occasion.

I will make a further attempt. Certain stars or
comets appear to grow progressively less distinct
before our eyes; but it does not follow
that this appearance is absolute. The fault
need not necessarily obtain within the observer's eye,
nor indeed upon that star; it is quite possible
that the relative motion of two systems subtly
has introduced a measureless distance in between.

Do you understand, or not?

Rotten posts are painted;

gilded nuts taste dry.
In secrecy . . .

Listen! There are sapphires,
garnets, amethysts, and many another jewel in Ceylon
where the king Sendernam wears a ruby
larger than a plum;
and we have seen it, my brothers and I,
and have shielded our eyes from its opulence.

What should I say next? I am held in thrall
by a thousand things.

As I walk past a woman's window
I hear someone whisper,
Lhurda, the dawn is breaking! It will soon be day.
My love, the dawn is here.

I have concealed myself.
I listen
while she remembers
mysteries of birth and creation.
I see her
entering the water,
who is
more wholly precious to me than wading animals,
or the swift iridescence of shark fins flecked with spume.

How should love endure two bodies' access gained?

I will not forget this enclosure—dark vines
and the smell of olives, stone walls
of Moorish make, aloe, cactus, wild thyme, voices
hopelessly calling. It has been like this
since I can remember.

The palms are stirring,
the moon is down.
I will leave this place and rest
when I have come to Obydos.

In the depths there is no light
but that within.

I abandon myself to further contemplation.

Lat. 23.16 S.; Long. 90.10 E.
Mid-afternoon. The wind has veered.
The ship rolls and plunges.
The water grows dark and menacing.

From the bow of this vessel
moments ago I looked down and discerned
a gigantic presence
gathering form, rising toward me;
and I would have swum down to embrace a shadow
but that I felt myself embraced,
as though I were some mute pelagic beast.

Promises seldom, if ever,
are given to those at sea.

The octopus can not be imagined in any other way
except as the symbol of Evil.

There was a time when the Southern Cross was visible
from England.

Bjarni Herjulfson, having resolved to spend one winter
in the company of his father, who was in Greenland,
set sail out of Iceland. But a storm came up

and drove him to the south and west—he did not know
how long. When the storm had ended he raised his sail
and bore northward along a foreign coast, which was
the place we call New England. Herjulfson, because winter
was almost over, did not pause; having vowed to pass
these months with his father, in the year 986 A.D.

Near the close of the 15th century
the wine-dresser of Belvedere caught a lizard,
which he presented to Leonardo da Vinci,
who constructed out of the skins of other lizards
two miniature wings, filling them with mercury
so that they moved and trembled when the lizard walked.
And he made for his pet a little beard and some horns,
and kept it in a box; and it gave him pleasure
to offer his friends this grotesque creation.
To think deeply right now would terrify me.

A brooding spirit wraps each legend in loftiness
and grandeur. I will pursue this no further.

I think of Actæon, hunted by his own dogs.

All day I have meditated on the association of the dog
with Death. The dog has vast comprehension
and empathizes to a degree no human mind accepts.
When I was a child I was given a dog for a pet,
which one day got to its feet and looked at me and
barked three times in a way I never had heard.
Presently I was told my sister had gone on a voyage.

Animals, in their symbolic manifestation,
achieve life in the dim regions of the human soul.

To the horse, from time immemorial, man has attributed

supernatural properties. There are clairaudient horses,
those which are clairvoyant, and others which are able
to find the way when the traveler has become lost.
Horses exist that have mantic power. Horses prophesy
evil and divine treachery. They hear the words uttered
by corpses on their journey to the grave; but humans
cannot hear such words.

Patterns may be formed that fall apart
like crystals when a kaleidoscope is turned.

Adequate knowledge assumes its form.

I have just now remembered that I once fell asleep
in the mountains of Corsica. In a little while
two women appeared, riding a stallion without a saddle.
This animal turned its head in order to stare at me;
then the women, looking down, discovered I was there,
and as they kicked their heels the giant beast reared
like some heraldic myth, so that I thought of
monstrous carnivores which I have studied
in the pages of my Latin bestiary. Indolently I
gestured to them, whose hair streamed outward,
calling the various names which are meant for women,
hopeful that one might respond. I beheld them offering
white, alarmed faces. But the only sound was of hooves;
and I wakened to tremendous reverberations
as August thunder crashed through Corsican valleys.
I cannot begin to guess the meaning of this.

Each detail I have loved, for its own sake.

I must order my life after that of Saint Simeon Stylites,
who preached from the top of a column for many years
and made this place his home.

Every prayer I unite with some other,
that in such a way countless voices
raised in a multitude of accents
may join, creating a single invocation.

As thou
to me, so I . . .

Galileo Galilei
invented a thermometer, the pendulum,
and the hydrostatic balance.
Furthermore, it is generally assumed
he formulated the law of falling bodies,
constructed a telescope,
learned of a ring about Saturn,
the spots of the sun,
and the phases of our planets.
Because of these achievements
he was cruelly scourged.

There was a time in history
when the properties of anyone who had been
convicted of witchcraft were granted
to that man's accuser. No one doubts
this has its parallel in our day,
as credulity burgeons within calamity,
or we oppose each other;
since the relationship of our intelligence
toward the truth is not unlike that
of the polygon which is compared to a circle.
That is to say, resemblance may be increased
by the addition of numerous angles
to the former, but extended through infinity
still it cannot equal the latter.

Pius VI spoke approvingly of torture.

John Huss, the Czech heretic,
having been provided safe conduct
by the Council of Constance
to state his position,
was seized and burnt.

In previous days it was assumed
that each of our misfortunes must be due
to machinations of the Devil;
and if we could simply determine
some method by which to rout him
our sufferings would be alleviated.
Now another truth obtains,
since we presume that once our wings
have been spread across each Adversary
we shall live in peace and bounty,
while future ages commemorate
the prodigal alacrity of these days.

Have spent this morning in the archives
studying ancient manuscripts,
reflecting on the nature of our entertainment.
Neither crocodiles, nets, lustful beasts,
nor tridents appear remarkable in this context.

Ours is a world badly requiring that stately
grave nobility which is stamped on certain men,
like the colophon we expect at the end of valuable books.

In the science of mechanics it is axiomatic
that when various heavy bodies
act against each other

the resultant motion constitutes
the inevitable direction of their descent.

Now, we know that children are given to alarm
when they first learn how the earth and each planet
circumnavigate the sun, and stars go unfixed
within the limitations of the sky.
As they grow older they realize no calamity impends,
for as they fail to grasp the most natural laws
of the universe, yet they accept without hesitation
the deductions of their predecessors,
as sidereal magnitudes exceed our comprehension.

On the last day of June in the year 1908
in the forests of Siberia a noise was heard
louder than a thunderclap. A column of fire
surged upward and spread in every direction.
Trees were scorched of their foliage,
falling in vast concentric circles
from the omphalos of catastrophe. Reindeer
by the thousands, which had been feeding nearby,
were immolated—their antlers
and smoking bones a grisly testament. It is known
that on this date the Ponns-Winnecke comet
was less than three million miles from earth,
and there is reason to assume a minor fragment
of this excitation was responsible. But if so,
the question remains as to whether this cataclysm
in the forest should be regarded as an accident,
or whether it was intended as a warning.

Each step we choose is ours because of the one preceding.

Whatever we have derived from the past soon shall be
manifest. Time foreshortens.

Cinders discolor a wall: *Mene, Mene, Tekel* . . .

Kingdoms are numbered when they are finished;
prayers told for us are handed down too late.

My eldest son has inquired as to why, each mid-winter,
we gather religiously, and decorate a tree with
gaily colored strands. I have explained to him
that our ancestors, crouching in the low twilight
of Germanic forests, in order to placate brutal gods,
tied to the boughs of evergreen trees the bloody entrails
of their victims; and therefore we, obligated to our
deepest atavistic fears, follow the hideous custom,
seldom wakening from our monotonous dream.

Some say it is beyond the power of Man
to create, and he is fit only for destruction.
But yet I have heard of two men
left on an island to starve, and of how
at the approach of Death, one instructed the other
to feast on his body. Now, when he had died,
the survivor, contemplating the corpse, made ready
to cut up the flesh and devour it. But suddenly
his left hand reached forth and grasped his right hand,
which held the knife, proving he was not alone
as he had confidently supposed.

Purim.
The sky is dark.

One thinks of how slight and frail our hands become,
of how quickly they are wearied
and what little time is ordered them to play.

We know that we have our childhood with us always,

because it must be as Saint Augustine has written;
if it were not here, whither could it have gone?

Each year and hour foretell
the parabolic course of faith and life,
and death which is, or was,
if all that seems most real about us
comprise the thinnest substance of a dream,
till the heart be touched.

Travaille, regarde ton saoul
et le clocher a jour de Saint Pol,
et les belles œuvres des compaignons,
regarde, aime le bon Dieu, et tu auras
la grâce des grandes choses. And thou
wilt have the grace of great things.

We say of Jean de Meung
poetry and alchymy were his delight
and priests and women
the measure of his abomination.

These thoughts arrive more suddenly than swallows
troubling the air of a medieval tapestry,
continuing out of themselves. I will follow them
to where they go, and imagine the palace of Potemkin
which he built of ice to please his mistress,
which glittered night and day across Asiatic distances
until one warm breeze drifted through the south.

Who has argued that abstinence may prove advantageous?
Consider the Pope, who commanded fifty harlots
sent to his chambers, where his children danced with them—
Cesare and Lucrezia, removing their garments
for the sake of greater satisfaction. Lighted candles

were placed on the floor and chestnuts scattered
so that fifty naked whores crawled ecstatically
among the votive lights, eating nuts and copulating
for the sake of prizes.

The mind of Man is purged of vice in the same manner
as Metal is purified of dross. That is, through fire.

As for Roger Bacon, we know how his acquirements
so far exceeded the limits of his contemporaries
that they could account for such learning
only by supposing he was indebted to the Devil.

The exact number of the Devil's lieutenants
amounts to 7,405,926. This figure has been established
and found to be authentic. Somewhere in Germany
the Devil's own grandmother, a woman not altogether bad,
is alive and is reputed to carry nine hundred heads.

The extent of Hell is two hundred Italian miles
in breadth. This may seem too small. But reflect:
each cubic mile contains one hundred billion souls.

In the year 1450 the proposition that witches fly at night
became officially recognized; and with this presumption
the accused could not, through any means, give credence
to her innocence. For, if she were noticed at one place,
the accuser need only answer well and good, yet she flew
to the Sabbat where I beheld her. Five hundred years
have passed, and yet human credulity does not abate,
nor the need to inspire ourselves by usages of fright
and play witness to each extremity.

Françoise Secretain has revealed that in order to attend
the Sabbat, she places a white stick between her legs;

and uttering occult words, she is borne through the air!

Having sucked poison from another's system,
the whore is untouchable and a poisonous heroine.

Those which are guilty are boiled to death.

Faith is repugnant to reason.
Il faut opter . . .

As we go in search of the Jew
we preceed ourselves with a goose or a goat,
which animals are holy, animate
with divine power
enabling them to discover the retreat of unbelievers.

She recently had dug up, we judge, from the churchyard
her child's body and made use of it in magic compounds.
The husband argued that she was not guilty, saying
we had but to open the coffin and there we should find
the little body intact. Because justice is our reason
and we are inclined to mercy in every case, we proceeded
to the churchyard, where we had the grave unearthed
and the coffin opened. True, we saw the facsimile of
a corpse. So perfectly did it resemble an actual body
that none of us could have said this was an illusion
created by Satan, had we not been always conscious
this woman was guilty of her crime. This is the reason
we have burnt her; and because he was bewitched
we have burnt the husband also. The people give thanks
for their salvation; they praise us who have so
rid their community of foul magic. From here we travel
to the Auvergne; but where we will be found when we
have cleansed and scoured Auvergne, no one can say.

Daily we expend ourselves with hammering against the sea.

The essence of Woman lies with her corpus;
Man is made of the profiles of his face.

Each adept is required to choose another name
the instant he has accomplished the Magnum Opus.

Visions are not without their usage,
however fanciful,
if only to purge us of dark and sickening forms.
Faciat hoc quiquam alius, quod fecit . . .

We exist in an epoch cursed by Protestant armies
more insane and terrible than the black monks of Zaragoza.
This I state without fear of contradiction.

The hour is past eleven.
Pray for us.

I remember a vine-covered wall—the vines
oddly mutilated, the stones chipped
from the impact of countless bullets, whose magic
I have not yet quite forgotten,
nor the directions men choose as they fall.
I remember best that it was the month of August
and the earth was dry. Because this summer
has been so hot, I reminded myself—because
the dust is impervious, the earth will not accept
my brother's blood, for a little while.
To what prayer will you listen, if not to this?

Urban has preached a new crusade.
How many of us shall see our homes again?

When my son returned from the war he remarked
that the enemy so had committed and obligated him
that he was not able to spare one; thoughtfully
he explained how this weighed against his soul.

Murder may be regarded as a venial peccadillo,
so powerful is the influence of others.

I have tried to be content with the register of God;
where the heart leads, we follow.

A majority of Demons walk by night, since then
they easily pass into the heart of a man; but there is one
which is so bold he stalks through the heat of day,
and this we call the Demon of the Meridian.
Thus, the meaningful separates itself. Interpretation
shall be left to others.

Jura naturæ sunt immutabilia.

Peruvian women, without bitterness, offered their bodies
to victorious Spaniards. Not one
singly, and then another, but in unison
they acquiesced,
as rudimentary creatures seek passage to the sea.

Women gathered outside the Circus Maximus
to intercept the men who returned
from watching these bloody spectacles.
At such a time, no man was strong enough
to resist the supplication of lecherous whores.

During the Franco-Prussian war
the cannonade emanating from the Bois de Boulogne
attracted great multitudes of women

who arrived by landau and barouche, staring
at the guns, and got as close to them as they could.

Truly, the essence of woman lies with her corpus.

The Bear, unlike other beasts, does not copulate
after their fashion, but in the manner of humans.
Taken with each other, they join in a fierce embrace.

Concerning the Partridge,
desire so torments the female
she becomes pregnant
if even the odor of the male
carries to her on a breeze.
But this cannot be true of Woman,
who is above every bird.

The dung of the Cocodryllus
when employed in the form of ointment
makes aged and wrinkled whores beautiful,
and restores the vigor of youth.

Somewhere, I believe, I will meet my love again.

In a window across the street the curtains
have moved.
A withered hand appears,
and the features of an old woman
near the glass. She allows the curtains to fall;
I awake to the beneficent touch
of my mother's hand.
Is this a portent of things to come?

Slowly the carousel revolves. Painted stallions
rise on gilded spits,

descending while I dream
of Tancred
and an early love. Often enough
have I pressed the sweetest meat! — sweeter
than a wild fig! O I will ride back again
if she is there,
employing the phrases of Plantagenet kings!

Poems seldom are made but partially,
and honeysuckle
blooms at mid-summer.

How shall I abjure
what gives me pleasure?

It is bright and warm today.

Thou art thy mother's glasse
and she in thee
calls back the lovely
Aprill of . . .

Shadows fly overhead,
the field is darkened and
winds increase!

What has most deeply imprinted itself on my soul,
which has been most painful and enduring,
so that I have yet to shut it out of memory,
is the letter I received wherein
you demanded to know how many Germans
I had slaughtered, ordering me to kill
as many as possible, out of my esteem for you.
I have wondered, therefore, if it may not be
as I have heard, that each exceptional woman reveals

mental or anatomical characteristics of the male,
and vice versa.

If it should trouble you that I am whatsoever I am,
only remember I meant you no harm.

For now I will say only that night had fallen
when we reached the village
and the odor of Death was everywhere. A voice spoke
out of the shadows, to me, as I walked past,
saying: *Who are you? Why are you here?*
Tell me, if you can, how I should have answered.

What remains, finally, of precepts and didactic teaching?

A dog that is accustomed to lick blood in a butcher shop
is difficult to cure of this habit, and will return
even though he is pelted with stones. So is it with us,
which is the reason for discipline, whips, and cilicia.

I remind you of women, how frequently they dream
of the sun, blanched and swift, which enters their mouth—
the hope and eternal precognition of their sex.

I attempt to liberate each woman that I meet,
but on every occasion I am defeated
by those frantic and deceitful means they employ
to remain in bondage. They have not altered in centuries;
my amazement will never diminish. Still the cedars
are growing in Lebanon, and wild figs are sweet.

Whatever I set down is true. If this truth
should contradict some other, what is that to me?
If any man protests I have confused him, is the fault
his own, or mine? I am like those boughs of Austria

which gain eloquence when they are masked with salt.

Last night the villagers once again knocked at my door.
It was long after midnight, the fire in the athanor
was smoldering, and my familiar had gone to sleep.
I was at work, and it seemed to me I was nearer than I
ever had been to that stone for which we have searched.
This is why I shouted at them, so that they wept and
tumbled over each other in fright, and hurried away,
gesturing feebly. Who has given them the right to ask
why I refuse to lead a procession I have engendered?
I might have answered. Yes, I could have replied
that it does not concern me, merely the direction
it was meant to take. Now, regarding myself, other paths
appear more promising.

Avicenna of Bokhara has not died, as many suppose;
he has become immortal through the virtues of an elixir
made by his own hand. He will be found in a hermitage,
where he labors toward the solution of those problems
which beset us.

Leibniz was the last man to possess some knowledge
of the totality of human endeavor.

Columbus scribbled frenzied notes on the margins of
a manuscript by Marco Polo.

Peter Lombard considered it possible
to have intuitive knowledge, not only sensitive but
intellectual, of things which do not exist.

Someone is observing me! — I have sensed his presence.
If I acknowledged him, he would smile quickly,
offering factitious attitudes meant to assure me

of his respect, his measureless admiration; but then
he would proceed to catalogue such errors as he feels
are manifest. To confound him would not be difficult,
yet I should feign humility, knowing of a higher source.
In this, the elder Cato would confirm my choice.
From a fool I have much more to learn than he from me.

I have just this instant learned that in the year 325
a method for determining the supposed date of Easter
ultimately was established, and declared official.

This is the 29th of February, auspicious for those
who desire a glance at futurity.

I am chilled and sick at heart. Our time is almost here.

What kept me silent for so long? I could have spoken.

Lemons betoken the final separation.

By one folded leaf,
a twig bent,
note where we have gone.

Out of ashes,
voices speak.

Like all damned disciples of the Devil,
Agrippa died with his face pressed to the earth.

It is said that an angel appeared to Flamel,
carrying a marvelous book beautifully engraved
and bound in copper, its text traced out
with an iron burin; and the angel commanded him
to contemplate this book in which he understood

nothing, for its characters were indecipherable,
and told him that he would one day find in it
what no others could see. At these words
Flamel stretched forth his hands,
but the angel disappeared and where the book had been
Nicholas Flamel witnessed glorious floods of gold
rolling forth on the path they had taken.

Choose of some unknown thing any quantity that you wish.
Thus commences the formula by which
each alchymist accomplishes the Magnum Opus.

Cold winds across the Gulf. I am restless
and not at ease. Toward noon
the sun grew visible.
I have been here too long;
I will travel north, I think, as soon as winter ends.

Rumors of sulphur in Iceland.
I will go there to earn my fortune.

Because it ascribes to Jesus in the hour of His extremity
a pronouncement of bitter malediction,
Christians grow uncomfortable and seek to refute
the legend of the Wandering Jew.

This day have been let of twelve ounces of blood.

God the Avenger
sees all.

In a remote valley of the Caucasus
live the Khevsoor, descendants of Crusaders
led by Godfrey of Buillon, whose army,
while attempting to reach the Holy Land,

216

was shipwrecked on the shores of Turkey.
The Khevsoor wear helmets and chain armor
hammered of links, gauntlets and greaves
which are badly weakened and rusted.
Each time they emerge from their valley
the Khevsoor carry the double-edged sword
of their ancestors, and marvelous shields
which are circular and made of leather.

Those who are blind are not able to see.

Kubilai Khan on no account permitted the Cross
to be carried in front of him, saying
it was on a cross the son of God was tormented.

Marco Polo speaks of two Tartar kings of the 14th century
whose names were Toktai and Noghai, and of how
they decided to do battle against each other. Kings
address their armies. So speaks Toktai:
We have come to fight against King Noghai
and his men, with good reason. For you know
this hatred and bitterness has arisen because Noghai . . .
Thus speaks Noghai: *Brothers and friends*
we have won many battles and dreadful encounters.
May this knowledge strengthen your assurance,
together with the fact that right is on . . .

This soliloquy is composed out of whatever I say
to myself; there is no doubt of its absolute authenticity.
In good time I shall write of nebulous regions
within the air, of the formation of clouds,
the causes of snow and of hail, to say nothing of
new shapes which snow forms while it is falling, or
of trees I have studied through long hours
in cold countries. For now, I will set down that

Crimean Tartars hurled the bodies of plague victims
over the walls of Italian forts, and that Acestes
shot an arrow with such force it caught fire in the air.

I put down that an afreet was tamed by Solomon
and grew submissive to his will.

I further state that Francisco Pizarro
was abandoned on the steps of a church. He was nourished
by a sow, without which he would have died. This
I have written carefully, because of its importance.

I employ the procedure of Saint Gregory, which allows
for the sake of the moral a juxtaposition of all things,
no matter how incompatible or contrary.

I wish to mention that when we had dug some distance
into the hillside we unearthed crenulate battlements
of a wall that once had ringed the fortified city.
We knew, then, we should come at last to mosaic tiles,
pendants of glass and agate, carnelian beads
and crystal bowls, sapphires, rubies, and those
fallen columns we have learned to dread infinitely more
than a promise of Heaven, or the threats of Hell.

And we found, also, just at dusk,
the helmet of a Genoese crusader buried in sediment
eight centuries. We prayed for him.
In future times, who will attend to us?

I mention that Etanna was spirited to Heaven by an eagle
which pointed out to him the diminishing earth.

I remind you of the asteroid Eros,
twenty miles in length and five in breadth,

which periodically tumbles past the earth.
Whoever flings a stone from this mountain
will not observe its descent.

Life is short, art is long; occasion is volatile;
experiment is fallacious; judgment is difficult.

I call to your attention, so that you do not forget,
the oval door by means of which the sacrifice enters,
the windows for spectators, and beneath the chair
a shallow basin we are accustomed to fill with acid.

Someone wishes to know
in how many places have I lived,
in what omnipotent cities,
and the number of my centuries.
Shall I answer or keep silent?
When was it we sang for joy?

My master went to Esslingen, but I
was detained elsewhere.
Three hundred years later
I found the house where we had lived.
He had covered the chimney and the roof
with symbols; but of our tenancy
nothing remained, except
one hammer. Daily we expend ourselves
with hammering against the sea.

I must establish an image whereby each man may judge.

A certain bishop of Geneva burnt five hundred persons
in three months. A bishop of Hamburg immolated,
all told, six hundred. A bishop of Würzberg
burnt nine hundred, and the stench hangs over that city

to this day. Ten thousand were sent to the stake
by Torquemada, and the population of Spain decimated
by fourteen millions during a period of two centuries.
It is true that we yearn for annihilation. The earth
shall revert to worms and the rolling sea to plankton.

Hanukkah. This day encountered a Protestant
I mistrust.

I have just now met the double of myself
whom the Germans call Doppelgänger
which is a positive sign of approaching Death.
Tomorrow I shall waken myself earlier,
and earlier each morning,
there is so much yet to be accomplished.

Before it is too late I wish to set down that
throughout history Christians have been a source of wonder
in that they, more than others, always have been subject
to physical convulsions. I will further mention
that evidence suggests Jesus Christ was born in early
autumn, his birth being announced as the 7th of January
in an effort to obliterate the pagan feast of that date
by gilding it with a Christian myth. Much later,
in the 4th century after his death, the date was
changed again, since an important Mithraic celebration,
inimical and profoundly menacing to the Holy Fathers,
occurred on the 25th day of December.

Hunters make use of the lunar calendar;
farmers employ seasons of growth.
It is time to make the most of Winter;
who can announce the date of Spring?

Gnomic words record how sorrows end.

The most savage account which ever was written
concerning Mankind, we regard
as a book principally suitable for children!

My friend, the scholar, speaks often of the Bestiary,
which is a book that seems altogether as quaint to us
as we in our devolution shall seem to our progeniture.
That they, in their promised assignment, who delight
in their modernity, must meet with our extinction
seldom reflects his point. The Bestiarist informs us
that fish in the ocean depths cannot escape violence
from the power and inclinations of their kind; thus
the smaller are subject to the greater. One falls meat
to another, which results in this situation: when one fish
has swallowed another and is itself swallowed by yet
another, then it happens that both have come to their end
in one encompassing belly, the devourer and its devoured.
The Bestiarist further tells us this is no accident,
but is given us for our edification, as the fish has been
created by God to serve Man in the nature of a parable.
The moral, therefore, must be so construed: Whoever
has not done toward others as he might wish be done
toward him, then sooner or later he will be devoured.

There are three recognized attitudes of prayer.
The first is the lowest, as it is the most common.
It may be called Petitionary, because in this
we raise up our petition. The second, or Intermediate,
concerns intercession on behalf of others.
The highest is Identification with a Conscious Being.
This far exceeds the limits of comprehension.

Numerous pages in the autobiography of Emma Galgani
contain mysterious annotations, as if some individual
had attempted to cancel out the dignity of certain lines.

These curious intrusions cannot be removed; chemical
analysis fails to resolve the nature of their origin.
Theologians attribute these marks, which are not unlike
a musical clef or signature, to diabolic intervention.

The Wandering Jew, it is said, appeared
three centuries ago to a British invalid,
curing this man of some affliction.
English divines began at once to investigate,
and to dispute among themselves whether
this manifestation had been of God or
the Devil.

It was customary during previous ages,
when all specified devils had been withdrawn
from a sufferer's body, to exorcise him
totally, after which salvation he was set afire,
because it was felt the soul had been infected.
This, furthermore, gave great satisfaction
to the populace. Words for the present hour.
Crescit cum magia hæresis, cum hæresi magia.

I must read deep into the *Malleus*
to discover our future through the past.
From multiple ledges of perception we depend
not unlike icicles which form in the warmth of winter;
finally fused, we present ourselves, one intricate mass
incredible to behold.

Now it seems I am standing before a small wood sculpture
of Saint Bruno, who is contemplating the Cross.
He is simply gowned in white, yet ornamentally,
and the cowl of his habit has fallen back.
His head is shaved, the tonsure three-quartered
Ike a laurel wreath, one tuft in its center.

I cannot imagine what this signifies, and I think
I should ask the artist who all morning
in a shadowy corner has been copying
some obscure madonna. But when I turn to him
he has gone, and I behold my sister joyously
playing with her first-born child.

What is important to notice in these prayers
is that they have no object to which or to whom
they might be addressed.

The wind blows from the east. Clouds stream overhead.

I have yet to find Him among images of corporeal things.
I wonder that He has vouchsafed to dwell within us, even
in our furthest memory.

Perhaps I should think of the village of Arae,
where a great king lives
whose name is Tatarrax, who prays incessantly, reading
the Book of Hours, and worships a woman,
the Queen of Heaven.

Illusion is brief; repentance bitter.

It has long been known how Bernal Díaz fell asleep
near Vera Cruz, and lost out of his pocket eight seeds
from which sprang those trees that later
were to bring forth the celebrated orchards of
Nurio de Guzmán, Viceroy of New Spain. And there are those
who say that even now, three centuries after,
certain trees of Mexico have descended from the seeds
lost by Díaz; and they bear a fruit too singular
for any mortal tongue. Of this I speak, of things
which germinate in darkness.

I have considered each accomplishment, and conclude
I am not unlike Amphiaraus, who foretold calamity,
but proceeded in company with the doomed and was
swallowed up by the earth. As helpless as he, I have
beheld falcons reel above the rock-bound coast,
seeming to observe us during the enactment of our
predestined ritual, which is more stringent
and more liturgical than Hans Holbein's *Dance of Death*.

Ash Wednesday. There is snow on the mountain.
Through the lemon trees a light rain is falling.

I believe the path is concealed by rock and bramble
which has grown subtly yet inextricably around the heart.

Patterns form and fall apart.

We have created the homunculus and I
have seen the monstrous being. Forty days
the sperm lay buried in manure
and each day at noon the Master turned his magnet
across it, muttering foreign words.
Then, on the fortieth day
he showed me the resemblance of a man,
but it was transparent, without a corpus.
He told me we should feed the loathsome object
for exactly forty weeks, and all this time
allow it to lie in its bed of manure
in a continual and even temperature,
so that its every member might develop.
This we did, much against my will.
And it grew into a human child,
though much smaller than any born of Woman.
Now, my friends ask me to make one for them
that they may be as horrified as I.

I would do so for their admiration, except that
I am merely the apprentice of the Master,
and I am afraid.

Da amantem et sentit quod dico; whosoever loves
as deeply as I
will not fail to understand.

These things are sounded through Greek and Latin,
but still they are not either of these, being designed
out of this present second.

Sublime pride, the quintessence of Evil, was conceived
before our time.

Quem colorem habet . . .

I remember without difficulty how the cathedral
was destroyed. The south tower slid like shale
into a crevice; the octagonal rose window fell
not quite cautiously, and shattered, disintegrating
before it touched the ground. Nor have I forgotten
my brother, who stood at ease, watching—one hand
at his belt. I still see him, and the plumes he wore,
with April sunlight glittering on his gold helmet.
What seems to me, even now, more grotesque than
the actuality of his abominations was his laughter,
the delight one could read in his eye. Perhaps
he has found the paradise of which others dream,
and years must elapse before his act swing home,
spiraling down, bloodied and limp as a scrap of fur
tightly clutched in the knuckles of a Nazi falcon. Or
it may be that he has sensed within himself
some affinity toward the universe—some cognition
perpetual and wholly indissoluble. When he speaks,

which is not often, I feel his silence. If he had been
an animal, I think he must have been a white bear;
or if he was a fish, he must of necessity be one
that swims singly and with vast ease around oceans,
but is lost in shallow rivers.

Tempora mutantur nos et mutamur illis.
Thus alter the times, and we with them.

I could not explain to any man where I have gone;
although each step is the result of long probation,
and statements almost never are made but partially.

My brother tells of visiting the tomb of Mulai Reshed,
who conquered Morocco, whose strength was recognized
across the Mediterranean as far as the shores
of the Atlantic. I expected, therefore, to learn of
a glorious temple, of opulence I scarcely could imagine;
but he said the sultan was simply buried under a dome
of sun-baked mud beyond the red fortress of Rissani
on the bank of the river Ziz, near the ruin of Sijilmassa.
My brother said nothing else, and gradually I perceived
how the tomb of Mulai Reshed, the ruins of Sijilmassa
and the diminution of a river had become intolerable
symbols of the course and progress of his own existence.

May the Grace of God be upon us, and upon our heirs.

I must consider what to say next. We have only
a few more hours.

Copernicus died when Montaigne was ten.

The luminosity of Rigel is twenty-one thousand times
that of the sun.

Fray Marcos de Niza was versed not merely in theology
but in cosmography,
and in every known art of the sea.
This I choose to register in vermilion script.

During the final season of life
Cortés and Columbus, haunting the royal antechambers,
importuning those who once had been honored
to receive them, seemed very much alike.

Existence does not matter, only what is meant.

Some assert the earth is at rest,
but Philolaus claims it revolves around
the central fire
and has an obliquely circular motion
like the sun or the moon.

Now do you understand?

Plotinus writes that he has heard from a learned man
how the motion of the sun, the moon, and the stars
become the constituent of time,
and that he assented not to this,
for why should not the motion of each body
be its time; or if the potter's wheel run round
and the light in Heaven cease,
should there be none to measure this dancing?

Speculation on the nature of celestial occurrences
in common with liberal aptitudes seems idle and sinful
to those of negligible elevation. However,
the moon, the sun, and the stars, which are fixed,
mutually affect one another through their orbit,
causing in our earth a subtle flux and reflux,

not merely in the sea, but equally above our heads,
affecting everything which pervades the universe,
affording us this last chance toward redemption.

Seats in Paradise were sold for the 20th of May
in the year 1773 when it appeared certain
a comet would strike the earth; it being explained
that by special intercession on behalf of the populace
the priesthood had obtained a limited number of tickets.
Persons inquiring as to whom their tickets
should be presented, a question regarded as blasphemous,
were denounced as atheists. This, too, I have decided,
must be entered in the ledgers of remonstrance—
a pattern for history, the apologue of our time.

Through meticulous calculations we have learned
that one pint of water on the surface of the white
companion to Sirius must weigh twenty tons, or more.
How is it we neglect the song and bitter narrative
told us near midnight by our closest neighbor?

Factory walls have cracked,
chimneys stood against a barren Flemish dusk,
abstemious testament! What might have been
is not to be; thus we gather—
uneasy groups annotating the bone-bright sky.

To believe is to live by error; each hill unfolds
some further valley.

It is known that during the 16th century
the conquest of Mexico was simplified by the
hesitation of Motecuhzoma at the Vale of Anahuac,
together with the mysterious reluctance of his warriors
to defend their homes on Lake Texcoco.

Ultimately the Spaniards heard of the mild god
Quetzalcoatl, whose skin was fair
and who, some say, wore a beard
and floated out of the East on a raft of snakes, and
departing, vowed he would be seen again
in five hundred years. History is simpler than it seems.

Are we not lured eternally by cities to the north?

There are fish in the rivers of Quivira
longer than horses,
and every tree is strung with gilded bells!
Therefore we pause, listening
to the breeze.

Almejo has been struck by a savage arrow
dipped in poison. We hoped he might recover,
although the flesh rotted and dropped from his arm,
and the skin also, leaving sinew and bone open to view.
And he gives off a stench like a swamp and
not one of us will go near him. But we are sorry for him
because he always has been a true friend.
Shall I compare this life to a flash of lightning
which, quicker than I mention it, exists no more?

Mid-day. The fin of a shark is visible.
I did not realize I had been asleep
nor what I dreamt, nor why I am thus
rudely torn out of one world into another.
We lie becalmed, half a week from Java.

In the province of Maabar they will not admit as witness
any man that drinks wine, or any that goes to sea.

Years turn. Leaves fall in their season.

I must set down, before it is too late, the pink murex
my daughter this morning brought to me, naming
for my benefit each part. I scarcely listened;
not that this shell might be less lovely
than she presumes—but that her touch and voice,
the confident gestures of an infant hand,
proved almost more than I could endure.
Have we not lived deep-buried in the pages of
children's books, in a world of high moral fable
and fantastic adventure, in times to make our blood
run cold? Is it not incumbent upon each of us
to keep safe from the holocaust all that matters?

Have we yet prayed to see all beings, however numberless,
delivered to the opposite shore?

We know the Pythagoreans were accustomed to hand down
mysteries by word of mouth, not through reluctance
to communicate their philosophies, but in order that
things which were of great beauty should not be scorned,
or in any fashion exposed to the ribald levity of
insensate persons, who could not care for them.
In the same manner, if you should be here, I
would not hesitate to confide in you, rather than
address myself to you thus, distantly.

We have with us throughout our temporal lives
a feeling that the spirit of the dead wishes to remain
next to its body; for which reason we bury our bodies
underground, that we may continue our existence
undisturbed by ghosts out of the past.
For greater assurance, we roll a heavy stone
on top of the forehead, or upon the breast.
If any ghost should rise up, his foot is caught
by the wreath.

I profess to a Celtic fantasy of mind, which cannot be
mistaken; this I set down in violet letters.

By our eager desire to pierce through the curtains
of futurity we often neglect our blessing,
dividing presumption into study, making numbers
of exceptional account, yet meager course,
and waste our early lives, forgetting how ignorance
becomes a state. This I would not dare interpret.
Out of each meaning others rise in a similar fashion,
as shadows alter sculptured marble.

What is unclear?

We feel there is within each one of us
something which will not ever die. Our experience
and every dream conspires to counter revelation,
making us hold this fondly, as leaves touch
to their only tree, our one presumptuous hope.

Listen. Let me tell you once more.
Each Saxon child is educated from birth
to be, invariably, the first; and is instructed
to measure himself according to such regrets,
envies, and hatreds as he engenders!
So far as his companions despise or emulate him
is he to be commended and respectfully
addressed. This is the heritage I abjure;
this is why I seek another declination
and cannot hesitate for less than the sight of anemone,
asphodel, and black Greek olives, or the sea.

To dream of the ash-tree portends
a lengthy journey.
Lime predicts an ocean voyage.

Yew and alder
presage sickness to the young,
dissolution of the old.
Water-lilies imply danger.

A breeze rustles our sail, a dog barks across the water,
a child cries. I re-live the somnolent heart of August,
hearing again my sister's voice, the touch of black elm—
when it seemed the plenitude of life might overcome me.
I think often of the days of my youth, of feelings that
seldom come back anymore.

I hear down the long, uneven years
the winding of a strange horn;
and I see,
as I often have,
the troubled faces of my parents.

I wish to mention my father, who herded sheep in the
province of Estremadura; and record the fact
that he once discovered a copper bell of such dimensions
he could not roll it over. It was almost hidden by weeds,
he said, and of the church where once it had hung,
pealing the genesis of each day, there was no sign.
He spoke of this bell to no one in his village;
you, he said to me, are the only person I have told.
He ordered me to go and find it, just as Death carefully
reached down, and I first recognized the majestic power
of symbols. That is all I know, except that tomorrow
I leave for Estremadura—yet not to find a bell.
I go to ask who remembers my father, either his visage
or his name.

I must abandon each pretense.
I will begin once again.

In the year 269 a decree was issued
to the effect that a certain man who was called
Jesus Christ, thenceforth
should be considered divine.
In the previous century
following prolonged debate it had been decided
this man was born to a virgin!

There can be no doubt as to the natural vices
of women, which constitute avarice,
mendacity, and self-deceit.
It is clear they are attracted to their own destruction.
It is necessary to beat them, for the sake of
mutual satisfaction.

Those of a gloomy disposition avail themselves
of necromancy; those which show a luminous countenance
are devoted to astrology.

The punishment for adultery in Scotland
was public humiliation. So feared was this
that women chose to murder their bastard children,
preferring the risk of execution for infanticide
to the thought of their fornication being
common knowledge. The beginning of every thing
is small.

Corpora lente augescunt cito extinguuntur;
we live for a little while.

These past few hours I have spent in a darkened room
listening to concerti,
experiencing the recreation of moods so exalted
I never could have known them
without assistance. Thus we poise

and counterpoise.

The madness of one drives others mad.
Unius dementia dementes. . .

Napoleon's gunners, carrying dismembered cannon
over the Alps,
frequently paused to embrace and caress the frigid iron.

Dieu le veut! Dieu le veut!
Allons-y!

I do not know how long I was wandering across the field
seeking to recover what I had lost
when I stumbled upon the body of the Russian soldier.
At first I thought he was one of ours, but
then I noticed his coat, which was a different color,
and for this I was most grateful. I nudged him
with my boot, and struck him, tentatively,
across the shoulder, ready to flee at the first movement.
I was uncertain what to do when I heard
a not unfamiliar buzzing noise, and I noticed
green bottle flies avidly settling upon his mouth
in confirmation. He wore a yellow ring,
and because it glittered among the weeds
I removed it from his finger; but suddenly
it was transfigured into a sheaf of papers,
and I was reading with rapt attention a letter
to my wife, bitterly complaining that I no longer
could be positive who I was, yet still responding
with alacrity to each command. And the enemy
had been vanquished! Of this, now, I am not sure.
Perhaps I will understand when I have been
completely prepared; I have not gained the confidence
of animals, which come to drink and hunt

when they perceive nothing anomalous is there.

The taste of life is not bitter enough to please us,
which is the reason we make onerous decoctions
for ourselves, out of steep wormwood and camomile.

I am searching for . . .

History and poetry must be explored equally
if light is to be cast across those feelings, attitudes,
and motives precipitating our estate,
since one without its other is like an ocean fish
which is but dryly eaten. Such problems suggest
to everyone who feels impelled to contemplate them
a stately, eloquent style; a style imbued,
furthermore, with foreign riches for the sake of distance,
since we have known these shores and the sea around,
and are not soon apt to forget the noise of trumpets
or the sight of Jesuits marching upon the New World.

I hear a cock crowing in the Andes!

I was asleep, that is all.

If by tomorrow the wind holds
we should raise the Venezuelan coast.

There is reputed to be a place in the jungle
where a gigantic snake is kept
which feeds on monkeys, nothing else.
Parrots shriek and stretch their wings
each time they behold the spectacle;
for it is said that each monkey
when he first observes that drowsy, balanced mass,
commences dancing and capering, as though

in such a way—by good-humored effort—
he expected to placate Death. Is it not a fact
that the same might be said of us?

In certain seasons the gryphon appears,
but this creature is not as usually represented—
half-bird and half-lion.
My brother has seen the gryphon
and described it to me. It is like an eagle
but of stupendous dimensions, so that
without difficulty it pounces on an elephant
and lifts him high up into the air and drops him
and crushes him by his own fall,
and next is seen to sit upon the carcass feeding.
What meaning has this? Circles of light are cast
by a lamp; to explain is not to absolve.
I know only that where the gryphon is found, there
my brother grew enamored of a woman from the Indies.

We have beheld the cockatrice, the manticore,
the amphisbæna, and the owl and fox,
and have heard the shriek of the Sea Bishop.
What shall remain for us out of this desolate waste?
Will we ever be forgiven?

We will not endure.
Man of himself can not prevail.

To conceal old guilt, we incur the new.

From immemorial time Germany has been obsessed
by the legend of the Wandering Jew.

Venom nestles in the shade; the breath of oxen
improves the atmosphere.

Words of abiding truth are found
in documents from the Middle Ages.
It is there we learn how persons of bad character,
though not to be believed upon their oath
during occasions of common dispute,
should be accepted at their word when they vow
some person has bewitched them.
Fear of the Devil exercises greater appeal
than our love of God.

A letter from Danzic during the height of the Plague
mentions that whereas one might suppose
the prospect of Death should act as a deterrent to Sin,
desperate minds seemed encouraged to greater Evil.

Turius und Shurius Int . . .

Circles bend of their own accord;
our time has come.

The tongue protruded thickly out of the mouth
and was of a blackish color. The hair of the head
was stiff and white. Neither carbuncles nor boils
disfigured the body, but numerous green and yellow marks
were found on the arms and legs. When the abdomen
was cut apart, the lower orifice of the stomach
was noticed to be discolored by gall. From the spleen
to the rectum, the larger intestine was shriveled
and wrinkled, as were the liver and kidneys.
The uterus had contracted. The bladder was empty.
The heart had shrunk and was darkly befouled
with polypous blood—glutinous matter resembling tar.

Lalle, Bachera, Magotte,

Baphia, Dajam,
Vagoth Heneche Ammi Nagaz,
Adomator Raphael
Immanuel Christus,
Tetragrammaton Agra
Jod Loi. König! König!

I feel a sense of suffocation in my throat!
I need to lie down. I will rest for a little while.

There is an odor of incense here, of suppurating
flowers. Bats flicker through the twilight,
down the nave and aisle of the church—exquisitely
sensate, strangely blind. Nothing can be more subtle
than this, nothing more amphigenous, as fungi
parasitically bloom in our depths.

Pater noster, qui es in cœlis: sanctificetur
nomen tuum. Adveniat regnum tuum. Fiat voluntas tua,
sicut in cœlo, et in terra. Panem
nostrum supersubstantialem da nobis hodie . . .

He wore gray pantaloons, slit to the knee,
and carpet slippers. Elaborately
costumed guards supported him, grasping him
by the arms, as though he meant to escape.
It was clear he never contemplated this—
an expression of wonder, of vast absorption
lingered on his sallow, withered features. Truly
he did not understand; he could not guess
why he was here. Perhaps he thought himself asleep,
curiously delivered to our ritual.

He complained we had not asked his permission.
Someone was sent for, who explained the necessity.

We felt this should assuage him. He listened,
but replied there are those who describe cathedral walls
through the meticulous analysis of a single stone.
After much debate, and the hearing of
learned testimony from pontifical authorities,
we ordered him strangled, for it seemed his words
were treason.

Trahit sua quemque voluptas.

Those who saw through the gross delusion
kept their opinion to themselves,
arguing that they were not to blame;
and none addresses a multitude
against the fiery, rose-red persuasion of its glory.

In previous times the people grew excited by
their victims' look of alarm, attributing misery to
magic, in lieu of its natural cause. Words for
today.

As we do not follow the hand of the Magician, so deftly
it moves; in that same way do we fail to comprehend
the workings of our mentality, but gaze upon it with
mystification, remarking the least part of its unity.

All that is most horrible shall be found
closest to that which delights us—
the glow of precious jewels, dark night,
woods and gardens, nascent forms; the noise of water
stills the course of unknown things.
Immense are the treasures of gold and frankincense,
and every art is found in Circe's cave.

The people of Mayence built such a fire

for the immolation of twelve thousand Jews
that the lead of the windows and the bells
of Saint Quirius church were melted.

What is seen is comprised of things which seldom appear.

In the year 1313 the lepers of France were burnt
by orders of Philip the Fair.
Historical instances devolve upon our time.

According to Boccaccio, without heed of what is
decent or indecent, the people exist—guided
by their instincts—and do by day or night whatever
voluptuous inclinations prompt them.

Livy informs us of malice, with which we are covered
from head to foot, Ike the boils of a virulent epidemic.

Accompany me to several places in Vienna
and I will show you trenches filled with corpses.
There you may contemplate what you have adored!
Zellianelle Heotti Bonus Vagotha Plisos sother osech
unicus Beelzebub Dax! Komm! Komm!

I hear the monotonous tramp of Protestant boots
across the outer reaches of the Universe!
There is no sound much less terrible than this.

What is to be
will be.

J'ai été lâche; j'ai eu peur
de la vie!
This was the haunt of dreams that lied,
of visions that betray.

Michael Mayer, a celebrated physician of the 17th century,
has drawn up ordinances asserting
that our meditations surpass everything imagined
since the craetion of the earth. He believes
we are destined to accomplish the regeneration of Mankind.

Those ostensibly curious correlations between
propensities toward faith,
and violence of every magnitude,
are observed to be not curious in the least
when we have taken into account the knowledge
that for those who are able to admit
the immortality of the human soul
the mortification of our flesh cannot be thought
too frightful.

Hier stehe ich, ich kann nicht . . .

All today we have been under heavy attack
but have in turn inflicted terrible damage everywhere.
During the afternoon it began to rain.
A man crouching to one side of me reached forward
with extreme caution to pluck a flower—
I could not say what kind. Then I noticed how
the other men also were watching him.
He peeled away the petals, not brutally,
with a gentle movement born of patience and love,
or some immense familiarity; and we were transfixed,
our weapons as they were. When he began to speak
we knew, without knowing how, once he had been
a teacher of some sort—but of what,
none could guess. He did not find it strange to lecture,
nor did we. He pointed out to us the calyx,
which, as he explained, is made of green sepals;
the corolla, composed of colored petals;

the stamens, which bear the pollen; and the pistils,
at the base of which we find the ovary
containing the egg, or female element.
He explained how a tube from the pollen grain
grows down inside the pistil, and is responsible
for the fertilization of the egg. From this,
he said, fruit and seed are developed.
In a single flower, or separated in various flowers,
both sexes may be borne.

Certain truths we obtain are not ours
but through digression from the usual trend.

Do not forget that during the war a British nun
each day boarded a bus and silently paid her fare
with a brutal, hair-covered hand.

Shadows coalesce; hours
divide.

What remains of abominations
we have wrought?
What shall we crown with flowers?

For a long time I was troubled by their request
and considered it carefully, inquiring of myself whether
the remuneration, handsome as indeed it was,
might or might not allay the malaise I felt. I
discussed this with my wife, who replied
she would be content, if it were what I wanted.
Now, anxiously, without hope, I petition God,
having long since lost all but the vestiges of faith.
Why am I not able to keep my eyes from our catholic
ensign, where it arches toward the sun? All day
have I watched pale birds call ceaselessly! —

clapping their brittle wings as they float across
that gilded spire, sharper than any needle.

It is late;
we can only hope.

Has the author, Porson, begun his first book
concerning the details of human folly?
He has promised it ought not to exceed, at the most,
five hundred volumes.

Have we wearied of the letters of our name, until
we are no less nameless than a Gulf
or a terrace which has its name,
but in reality is cast of previous hours?

If, in the name of God, we thus employ our times,
tell me, when you have learned, the Devil's labor.

Out of grave necessity I create this rosalia.

I have been wondering if each individual
is possessed of his own wisdom, or if
whatever exists and is known
must be regarded as common to us all;
and therefore he that looks most rigorously
into mutual depths thus should be thought
least unwise. Perhaps I will ask the next man
that I meet, if he be not offensive.

There was a certain prince of the Tartars who,
having become a Christian, vowed he would go to Lyons,
there to kiss the foot of the Pope and witness
the sanctity of Christian morals. Louis the King
sought to dissuade him from this, being positive

that this Oriental, once he had viewed the true state
of Western affairs, must start back in revulsion.
But the Tartar would not be dissuaded and went;
and he came down from Lyons still more firmly converted
because, as he said, this must be a great religion
which can maintain itself when even its titular head
and its retainers are so sunk in depravity and evil.

Meaningful associations are formed
beneath our conscious level; this process
is like a dream.

Bodinus remarks for our edification
that whoever is accused of sorcery should not be
acquitted, unless the malice of the prosecutor
is clearer than the sun; for it is difficult to bring
proof of secret crime, and not one of a million
could be convicted if tolerant arguments were entered.

A saucer of new milk absorbs poison from the air.

The philosophy of those who exert their influence
on the opinions of butchers and fishwives
silently works its cure.

The comet of 1532 was excommunicated.

To each question are many false answers. But there is one
which is final. On this account, if none other,
I undertake, again, to communicate to you my thoughts.

Of the many hundreds, there was only one
who did not succumb, but held himself chaste.
He, also, was the first—a Jew of Italy
whose father carded wool, whose mother's name

was Susanna Fontanarossa, whose life was ended
in chains and disgrace, whose bones we have lost.

Francisco Pizarro chose
the sister of his most celebrated victim
for a mistress.

Bernal Díaz del Castillo reported a pyramid of skulls
arranged on the plaza with such symmetry
he had no difficulty estimating their number.

Passages are found
out of each into some other,
as we proceed through a sequence of caverns
between which filters a vague, prismatic light.

My father's estate and his books have been confiscated,
together with the sum of six million pounds,
notwithstanding that a special edict
had been drawn up during the period of his eminence,
declaring that his fortune, or any other thing
which belonged to him, could not be seized
by anyone whomsoever, for any known cause, or
on account of any conceivable circumstance
from that date forth, up to, and past the end of time.

Is it not a wonderful spirit I keep imprisoned
in the hilt of my sword?

Pentecost.

Two full weeks since we have seen any living thing.

Tonight we made out fires on the headland.
Some say these are signals meant to dissuade us,

since the moon is full and our sail
should be visible on the open sea.
Yet we turned no closer to land, nor can guess
what cape that was. Certain constellations of the south
lie ever higher; the wind blows cold, and it is
now a month, less four days,
since the captain's voice was heard.
Many think we have cast off toward some final port.

In a dream last night I found myself
swimming through turbid currents toward the bridge
of a sunken ship—to the ship's compass
which was encrusted with gem-like coral!
Its needle was pointing north, forty fathoms down,
and I was deeply awed; it had not wavered in
centuries. I would have struck the compass
to see it tremble, except that I dared not.
I turned and swam away into the fatidic darkness
from whence I had come.

I would search for the meaning to every occurrence,
if there were time.

The ship has changed its course;
eerily as it grows light
and swiftly dark again, we seem to hesitate, but then
advance with unutterable certitude.
Darker than before we plunge down yielding seas
eternally lashed by galactic winter rains.
The rain falls steadily upon us, day after day.

Through a rift in the clouds we have sighted a coast;
but there is a white-haired seaman who comes among us
winking and whispering it cannot be found on any map.
There are those who believe an error has been made—

an error of the utmost significance. All of us
are deeply frightened. We can only wait, placing our trust
in strange hands.

Two white gulls, driven apart, tilt across Chaldean winds.

Waves rush toward our gilded figurehead; the sky
looms black, and we
are not destined to solve the mighty riddle! *Pater noster,*
qui es in cœlis, sanctificet . . .

The enticing odor which comes out of the mouth of a whale
represents the lust of the flesh.
The jaws which close on unwary schools of fish
symbolize the Gates of Hell closing on the lost.
The mistake of a sailor who chooses evil for good, or
danger for safety, is the tragic error that leads
to utter damnation.

We listen fearfully to the noise of
cracking sails; we are carried onward, ever faster
through increasing darkness.

Ropes have been stretched taut on the deck;
without them not one of us could move, so steeply
does this vessel list.

The roar of waves is deafening us.
Rain blinds us.
If we but loosen our grip, we are lost.

I must put down my thoughts
like the vital signs of the Zodiac.

Frost shall freeze

and fire melt wood; earth blossom
and ice bridge the roof of water;
lock out budding growth.
Almighty God, winter shall pass
into spring, fair weather
return, and the sun
shine hot on the restless sea.

Lat. 58.10 S.; Long. 40.16 W.
Wakened by a shriek!
Some say it is morning,
I do not know.
The sails look hard as bone.
We bear always further South
and fast toward the glowing West.

I must be calm. All men have met distress. I
will meditate. What else
could preserve us?
Each life is the fruit of constant illusion.

Certain attitudes, feelings, and senses
I have not saved from the hecatomb, but yet
others have come readily
in unbroken and determined order; each that I have
summoned; and each
has given way, to whatever follows.

I will now contemplate the words of Saint Augustine
which I have embellished, which I set down
because of their inestimable worth. With piety
and devotion toward you, thus I commit his thought
together with mine, which are mutual, for safe-keeping.
These things do I within, in that vast court
of my memory. For there are present within me

Heaven, Earth, Sea, and whatever I could think therein,
besides what I have forgotten. There also meet I
with myself, and recall myself, and when, where,
and what I have done, and under what feelings.
There be all which I remember,
either on my own experience or other's credit.
Out of the same store do I myself with the past
continually combine fresh and fresh likenesses
of things which I have experienced,
or, from what I have experienced, have believed:
and thence again into future actions, events, and hopes,
and all these again I reflect on, as present.

What is the color of wisdom?
It must have the color of snow.

We have seen mountains fly toward us and pass beyond us
so that their pinnacles and canyons first
are illuminated by the sun, but then are in shadow.

One day this earth shall obey our command,
undertaking its journey toward the stars, lighted
by its own suns, which shall not dim
or go out, since we have built them out of the beauty
we possess, but seldom find.

Within the lifetime of one man
a ship that is made of iron can rust into nullity.
Inexorable currents sweep the depths
of anachronistic hollows. Without remission,
pray for us.

We course far ahead of the wind.
An odor of musty linen comes out of the hold.
I have met three seamen

who huddled in terror when I gestured to them.
Were they not able to see me?

I have asked everyone on board
if they know where we are bound. No one answers.
Of the captain—none has heard of him
since we raised the ice-bound cape.
I will ask the officer with the sextant. I
must find him, and ask
before he measures the night.

Another flag has been pinned to the chart; they tell us
we have nothing to fear
if we sail toward the hurricane's eye!

The moon is a rosebud floating out of reach
beneath the surface of the water.
Down phosphorescent valleys our strange ensign flutters;
we are aboard a funereal ship which has no port.
Waves gleam black, lapideous and menacing;
rollers stream toward us; dead foam
spins from the track of the scouring wind; we
are half-frozen. Privately the mate has whispered
that we cannot stay afloat; desperation engulfs us
as this vessel sinks toward the raging water.

Let us go not unrecorded.

Lat. 62.14 S.; Long. 90.24 W.
I believe . . .

Thus begins the end.

I will preserve to the last
a stately, medieval faith.

Ominously
with monitory succession
circular waters turn
beneath our ship.
Waves we seldom see;
but yet we feel
their presence
and long for morning,
that if we drown
it shall be in the sight
of other men, who say
what became of us.

No one speaks. None looks upon the water.
There is a volume to the sea I have never known.

Do not call out that it was meaningless;
you have heard the warning.

We are full of anxiety. Space surrounds us and
shines through us until we appear luminous in the light
of other worlds.

My thumb, my pen, and my first finger
I have bound up like spears of wheat. The rain
and the wind and sea create
their trinity against us.
I have no further time to lose.

Isadore of Seville compiled a summary of
all human knowledge.

The body of Saint Thomas
lies in a town in the province of Maabar.

Albertus Magnus constructed
an automaton with the power of speech,
which inevitably was destroyed
by Thomas Aquinas.

The condition of life is defeat.

I must make one further attempt,
if there is time. Between the two stars which constitute
the binary called Algol,
the distance is six and one-half million miles,
one-fifth the radius of Mercury's orbit.

Early iconographies are redolent of the sea.

Nothing is born that does not pass away. *Deficit omne*
quod nascitur. I must establish . . .

It is too late;
I am overcome with knowledge.

Nothing must interrupt the course of these,
which are my supreme meditations.
Hæc tibi dona fero; here are my gifts.

The clouds have parted.
I behold, or believe I do, the great star
Epsilon Aurigæ.

Out of obscurity
Man shines more brightly.

It is said that I am a man, and nothing that relates
to Man is alien to me.

Lege,
quæso.

We are tranquil and resigned;
the bow is half-submerged.

The ship is rolling on its side; I look into the depths.

There is the sound of an organ somberly playing.
Seas obscure the ultimate miracle of Heaven.

The journey is almost ended.

What holds us here?
Why are we preserved?
There is no hope.

In this, our extremity,
I see how foolish we have been.

None remains. They
have gone.
I alone am left.

Keep thou, O Earth,
what men could not.

Magnus ab integro sæculorum nascitur ordo.
Thus the mighty cycle of the ages shall begin again.

Cede Deo
Submit to Providence

Printed in the United States
By Bookmasters